Calling On God

My Questions
&
His Answers

Calling On God

My Questions
&
His Answers

by Nancy Brower Keating

"He who belongs to God hears what God says."
(John 8:47 – NIV)

"My own sheep will hear my voice…"
(John 10:27 – TPT)

*"This is what the Lord says … Call to Me and I will answer you
and tell you great and unsearchable things you do not know."*
(Jeremiah 33:3 – NIV)

*"For revelation knowledge flows to the
one who hungers for understanding."*
(Proverbs 14:6 – TPT)

Book and description available on my website
www.callingongod.com through Amazon and Barnes & Nobel

ISBN 978-1-960133-16-8 (Paperback)
ISBN 978-1-960133-17-5 (E-Book)

www.callingongod.com was designed by
Lisa Saccoia (LisaSaccoia.com)

Printed by Glens Falls Printing in the USA

ENDORSEMENTS

I love Nancy's heart for God and his word. The pages of this book are sure to encourage and inspire, while also kindling a desire for an ever deeper intimacy with God. ❧

> Shay Mason, Co-Founder of Love Inside Out
> and author of *Rest for the Weary*

This book chronicles one woman's quest for greater intimacy with God, to hear His voice and truly know Him as Father. It is a must read for anyone seeking to know God and better understand His plans and purposes for our lives. ❧

> Joseph E Simpson, Former Director
> of The Open Door Mission

The tender, childlike heart seeking to hear from God is beautifully portrayed in the conversations Nancy & God shared. Each conversation in this book gives us an "up close and personal" seat at the table as God answers the heartfelt questions posed by Nancy. Each answer is supported perfectly with God's words in scripture. You will be touched as God intimately shares from His Heart His purpose & perfect love for each of us. ❧

> Debbie Geer, Founder & President of
> "Hope for a Woman's Heart" www.h4awh.com

Calling On God is a wondrous book in which Nancy shares her remarkable journey of seeking the Lord's answers to the issues of her heart. I believe it will reveal more of Jesus and His love to you. I believe it will bring His peace upon you and move you to close your eyes and rest in sweet meditations. And I believe it will bless you like you never would have imagined. Expect change! ❧

> Tom Wiedl, Intercessor and Former VP of
> Sales and WOW at a large Federal Credit Union

Every page of this personal devotional story of Nancy to her Lord is extremely revealing of the character, mercy, kindness and the holiness of our Savior Jesus. The precious comments from Jesus draws the reader into the anointing of the Holy Spirit to long and desire for more of Him personally. ❧

> Judy Wood, Intercessor

If you want to experience the depth of God's love, and realize the yearning of His heart for you, then read on. God takes great joy in seeing His children seek Him. Nancy Keating has been seeking God for many years and the result illustrated in her writings is like gold. Evident in her words and her life are God's promises, relentless love and devotion to us. Calling On God illuminates that His desire for His children, who are made in His image, is to desire Him as much as He desires us. ∾

Steve Stephens, Ambassador, Shalom Unlimited

This sweet yet powerful devotional provides nourishment for the soul. Nancy's collection of writings reveal the magnificent love and insight available to us when we commune with our Lord. Within these pages you will find rich scriptures and journal prompts to help guide you into your own private time with the Lord. You will be blessed! This is the perfect devotional for personal use, bible study or book club. ∾

Lisa Saccoia,
Freelance Social Media and
Digital Marketing Specialist

Calling On God goes beyond a morning devotion or your personal meditation on a scripture; it calls on God to hear His heart on a matter. Some of the questions Nancy asks God ring across all our lives, maybe yours. Watch and see what He would say to one who has taken time to listen, and you may find yourself wanting to do the same. Her questions are timely, at once personal and corporate, national and secret. Nancy records God's voice as if one Friend is speaking with another. Sprinkled with His wisdom and engendering confidence in the One who loves us, the overarching voice of *Calling On God* is, "Come to Me!" ∾

David W. Asher, D.O. and Intercessor

Nancy's gift to us of her private two-way journaling is priceless. Thank you for sharing your recordings from God's heart. May all who read this book be blessed, personally know the intimacy of hearing God's voice for themselves, and walk in His Shalom Shalom. ∾

Kay Loke, Intercessor and Bible Study Leader

FOREWORD

Calling on God by Nancy Keating reveals an astounding revelation: God wants to take walks with His children in the cool of the day and talk with them about the things that are on their hearts and the things that are on His heart. That is exactly what God did with Adam and Eve (Gen. 3:8). Unfortunately sin entered and broke up this beautiful intimate love relationship.

So in the fullness of time God sent His Son, Jesus to redeem mankind from the curse of sin and to reestablish communion with His children. Jesus modeled the lifestyle God had for us by doing nothing of His own initiative but only what He saw and heard His father doing (Jn. 5:19,20,30). Jesus stated: "My sheep hear my voice" (Jn. 10:27).

My problem for the first ten years of my Christian life was that I didn't know what His voice sounded like. Finally I felt led to take a year and search out an answer to this perplexing issue. Revelation flowed. I finally understood that His voice is experienced as flowing thoughts that light upon my mind. His visions are flowing pictures that light upon my mind. Jesus talked about this flow when He said, "'Out of your innermost being shall FLOW rivers of living water.' This He spoke of the Spirit" (Jn. 7:37-39). Flow! I did not have a theology concerning flow. It was time to build one. So I did.

There is a river that flows from the throne of God (Rev. 22:1). It flows into our hearts when we accept Jesus as our Lord and Savior. I have certainly had flowing thoughts during my lifetime that were exceptional but it never occurred to me to attribute them to the voice of God. Now I do. I also have come to understand that this flow is purified by where the eyes of my heart are fixed (Eph. 1:17,18). If I fix them on Jesus (Heb. 12:2) and ask Him a question and tune to flow, the flow most likely will be coming from Jesus. Of course once it is written down, I test it against Scripture and with my spiritual advisors (2 Cor. 13:1; Prov. 11:14). Once confirmed, I run with it.

Here are four simple, childlike steps which Habakkuk, the Apostle John, and others took:

1. I **quiet** myself down (Hab. 2:1,2; Rev.1:9-11)

2. I **fix my eyes on Jesus** whom I behold at my right hand (Acts 2:25; Heb. 12:1,2)

3. I **tune to His voice** (flowing thoughts) **and His visions** (flowing pictures). FLOW is the River of the Holy Spirit which flows within the heart of the believer (Jn. 7:37-39)

4. I **write out** this flow that I am receiving (Hab. 2 - 3; Rev. 1 - 22)
   A free overview of the above 4 keys is available at www.CWGministries.org/4keys

Summary: Hearing God's voice is as simple as quieting yourself down, fixing your eyes on Jesus, tuning to flow, and writing.

Nancy has used these four keys in her daily devotions for years. This book is the fruit of those special times together with the Lord. They will inspire you to try these keys yourself, so she has provided several blank pages in the back of this book for you to apply the keys and journal out what the Lord is speaking to you. Of course, you may choose to do this journaling in your own journal rather than in this book.

The important thing is that you commune with your Lord and Savior and receive His wonderful counsel on a daily basis. He is longing to commune with you! God sent Jesus to die on the cross for our sins so He could restore a relationship with us. How's that for a passionate love affair?

May you celebrate and yearn for fellowship with God as much as He yearns for fellowship with you.

Mark Virkler

Founder and President of Communion With God Ministries:
www.CWGministries.org

Founder and President of Christian Leadership University:
WWW.CLUonline.com

For more information, the book *4 Keys to Hearing God's Voice* is available at:
https://www.cwministries.org/4keys

INTRODUCTION

In 1975, my husband and I dedicated our lives to the Lord. I was 23, and Jim 27. Two years later we were married and within the next 5 years we were blessed with two wonderful daughters – and since then a wonderful son-in-law and grandson.

We've been students of the word for over our 45 years of married life, but up until 2012, I had a one-way relationship with the Lord – I prayed and talked to Him, but I never realized I could hear from Him!

The year 2012 is when that all changed. During a bible study, I was introduced to a study by Dr. Mark Virkler "4 Keys to Hearing God's Voice" and began the discipline of asking God questions and writing down what I heard Him say – not audibly, but in my spirit – the Holy Spirit to my spirit. Supportive scriptures are provided on each page, using primarily the New International Version and The Passion Translation.

In this book are questions I've asked God and answers I received from Him over the past 10 years (2012 – 2022). All along, in my heart, I knew these writings were not just for myself, but were to be shared with others – Christians and non-Christians alike. God wants all to know the great love He has for us.

A friend of mine who recently went home to be with the Lord heard God say: "Know Me, Know My Word, Know My Nature, and Know My Ways". Through these writings, I've become more acquainted with Him, His Word, His Nature and His Ways. I hope you, too, will become better acquainted with Him as well! Intimacy ("into me see") is His desire for each of us – to become intimate with Him. With this, I bend low and give all the glory to God who produced this work. I require no credit for it. With this book I share His heart with you.

Scripture:

I pray that the Father of glory, the God of our Lord Jesus Christ, would impart to you the riches of the Spirit of wisdom and the Spirit of revelation to know him through your deepening intimacy with him." (Ephesians 1:17 – TPT)

"…And may he express through you all that is excellent and pleasing to him through your life union with Jesus the Anointed One who is to receive all glory forever! Amen!" (Hebrews 13:21 – TPT)

TABLE OF CONTENTS

Endorsements
Foreword by Dr. Mark Virkler
Introduction

Call To Me 1
I Am With You Always... 2
My Overflowing Cup 3
I Am 4
Be Patient 5
Intermingled 6
Trust Me 7
My Ways Will Prevail 8
Live In My Love.. 9
I Am Your Burden Bearer... 10
Restored And Refreshed 11
I Will Lead You 12
With Me You Can Do All Things 13
Remember Me 14
I Am Doing A New Thing 15
The Time Is Short 16
Use My Name And Apply My Blood.. 17
Come To Me First 18
Learn To Trust Me More 19
Come And Find Your Peace.. 20
Me In You, You In Me 21
Live In My Abundance.. 22
Expect 23
I Long To Be Known 24
My Purposes Will Prevail 25
Learn To Listen More Than You Speak.. 26
I Desire To Do A New Thing... 27
I Will Rule And Reign Forever 28
Co-Operate With Me.. 29
Receive My Love As A Gift 30
Serve 31
What Is Written Will Be... 32
Freely Give... 33
I Will Not Return In Vain.. 34

Pray Unceasingly And Remain In Me 35

Put Me On Display...36

Come And Lean On Me 37

The More You Spend Time With Me,
the More You Will Look Like Me 38

I Am With You Always..39

A Gift Is Not A Gift Until It's Given Away..40

You Are My Hands, Feet And Voice 41

Be Not Afraid..42

I Love To Share My Secrets With You..43

Use Your Gifts And Use Them Well 44

All My Creation Is In Good Keeping With Me 45

I'll Never Leave You Nor Let Go Of You...46

I Have Appointed You For Such A Time As This 47

Drink Deep And Pour 48

He Is Coming Soon 49

This Is True Intimacy 50

I Have The Gift Of Abundant Life For You 51

Know That I Am With You Always 52

Extend My Love To Those Who Have Not Yet Found Me 53

Let Go And Live...54

Peace And Joy Unspeakable 55

You Are The Object Of My Affection..56

You Are On The Verge Of Breakthrough...57

I Am Bringing You Closer To Your Destiny.....................................58

You Are Not Of This World 59

Purposed For My Appointed Time 60

Love Like I Love You...61

Hear My Voice 62

Commune With Me...63

Co-Seated We Will Always Be 64

Apply My Blood and Live..65 & 66

There Is Peace In My Presence 67

I See You..68

With God, All Things Are Possible..69

A Reserved Place For You..70

I Love You 71

Journaling Pages

Lord,
I dedicate this
book to you
with a grateful
heart.

"CALL TO ME"

My Question:

I was meditating on the verse: "Call to Me and I will answer you and tell you great and unsearchable things you do not know." (Jer. 33:3 - NIV) So, I asked: Father, where did you come from?

His Answer:

I am the width of widths, the height of heights, the length of lengths and the depth of depths.

I am the Creator who was never created – The Designer who was never designed - The Lover who was never loved - The Principal who beset all principles.

I am the Beginning and the End. I hold the scepter, the ancient scepter in My hands. All days were created and flow from Me - that is why I am The Ancient of Days.

I Am that I Am that I Am...

Scripture:

"Can you fathom the mysteries of God? Can you probe the limits of the Almighty? They are higher than the heavens above – what can you do? They are deeper than the depths below – what do you know? Their measure is longer than the earth and wider than the sea." (Job 11:7-9 – NIV) "

...Before me no god was formed, nor will there be one after me." (Isaiah 43:10 – NIV)

"This is love: He loved us long before we loved him." (1 John 4:10 - TPT)

"Your throne was established long ago; you are from all eternity." (Psalm 93:2 - NIV)

"For the word of the Lord is right and true; he is faithful in all he does. The Lord loves righteousness and justice; the earth is full of his unfailing love." (Psalm 33:4,5 - NIV)

He said to me: "It is done. I am the Alpha and the Omega, the Beginning and the End..." (Revelation 21:6 - NIV)

But about the Son he says, "Your throne, O God, will last forever and ever; a scepter of justice will be the scepter of your kingdom. (Hebrews 1:8 - NIV)

As I looked, "thrones were set in place, and the Ancient of Days took his seat..." (Daniel 7:9 –NIV)

"I AM WITH YOU ALWAYS"

My Question:

Father, in Jesus' name I come to you and am waiting to hear a word from you.

His Answer:

Never let me out of your sight. I am with you always, and long for your fellowship throughout the day. I provide good counsel, and with me you can do all things. Learn to trust me and lean not on your own understanding. I will show you great and mighty things that are to come. I will take you to the heights where my light shines so brightly that the streets of gold reflect like a mirror all around.

I am with you. Remember me. Do not let me out of your sight, for when you do – danger lurks – but you are always safe with me.

Scripture:

"…And never forget that I am with you every day, even to the completion of this age." (Matthew 28:20 – TPT)

"…And the street of the city was pure gold, clear as crystal." (Revelation 21:21 – TPT)

"MY OVERFLOWING CUP"

My Question:

Father, as I still myself before you, tell me more about Psalm 23:5 "You prepare a table before me in the presence of my enemies. You anoint my head with oil; my cup overflows."

His Answer:

I am your provider in the good times and bad. As you look to me, I reach my heavenly hands earthward and show myself strong on your behalf. Yea, there are many dangers, but I am the one who goes before you preparing the way you should go. As you seek my face, I anoint you with my very presence. Seek and you shall find me. Knock and I will open the door and come in and sup with you. I will supply all you need and will refresh your thirsty soul. I will give you refreshment and strength – and you will go and refresh and strengthen others. This is my overflowing cup. You are my cup overflowing. Continue coming to me for all that you need. Come to talk with me and ask me all that your mind cannot conceive. My mind is higher than yours, and my ways are higher than yours. But you are not a foreigner. You are my very own, and I want to show you my mind and my ways. Yes, even these are overflowing as a cup. Come and drink of my overflow.

Scripture:

"You will seek me and find me when you seek me with all your heart. I will be found by you, declares the Lord…" (Jeremiah 29:13 - NIV)

"Ask, and the gift is yours. Seek, and you'll discover. Knock, and the door will be opened for you." (Matthew 7:7 - TPT)

"Behold, I'm standing at the door, knocking. If your heart is open to hear my voice and you open the door, I will come in to you and feast with you, and you will feast with me." (Revelation 3:20 - TPT)

"As the heavens are higher than the earth, so are my ways higher than your ways and my thoughts than your thoughts." (Isaiah 55:9 – NIV)

"I AM"

My Question:

Lord, reveal a glimpse of the Ancient of Days. What does it look like? What is it?

His Answer:

I am the Ancient of Days. I am holy and my hair is white as wool. When I speak, my voice divides the heavens. I am desirous of my people. I am a jealous God, and desire to be lifted up among all men. Many idolize things that should never be. I am coming soon, and I desire my people to be focused on my plans and purposes. Many are going about – to and fro – creating images of their own making. I want to be their only image. Imagine me and who I am. You are made in my image. Keep your minds and eyes and hearts fixed on me and I will show you more. Yes, I will even show you what is to come. I am "The Ancient of Days". I Am

Scripture:

"Yes, and from ancient days I am he." (Isaiah 43:13, NIV)

"…thrones were set in place, and the Ancient of Days took his seat. His clothing was as white as snow; the hair of his head was white like wool." (Daniel 7:9 - NIV)

"I am jealous for you with a godly jealousy…" (2 Corinthians 11:2 - NIV)

"BE PATIENT"

My Question:

Lord, even though you wooed me at an early age, there came a time where I wanted to go it alone for a while. You were so patient and waited for me to return. I will always be grateful.

His Answer:

Just as I patiently awaited your return to me, I ask you to be patient with those your heart aches for. I, by my Spirit, will draw them. I will draw all men unto me. I love you with an undying love, and know and love those you love. Be patient and come to me often. I am the Alpha and Omega – your High Priest – the lover of your soul. I am awaiting our wedding feast.

Oh, what a feast it will be!

Scripture:

"And I, when I am lifted up from the earth, will draw all people to myself." (John 12:32, NIV)

"I am the Alpha and the Omega, "says the Lord God, "who is, and who was, and who is to come, the Almighty."(Revelation 1:8 - NIV)

"You kissed my heart with forgiveness, in spite of all I've done." (Psalm 103:3 - TPT)

"We're all like sheep who've wandered off and gotten lost. We've all done our own thing, gone our own way. And God has piled all our sins, everything we've done wrong on him, on him (Jesus). (Isaiah 53:6 - The Message)

"INTERMINGLED"

My Question:

1 Cor. 6:17 "…He who unites himself with the Lord is one with Him in Spirit."

Lord, what would you say to me about this scripture?

His Answer:

Tune to me daily. Yes, turn your eyes toward me, and I will remind you of my very presence with you. Hold fast to me. As you speak, ask of me. I love how your lips shout out praises unto me. I am intermingled with your very voice and spirit. I am in your nature and essence. Ask of me often throughout your day. Talk with me – I am with you, and long to converse with you. I love to counsel you and lead you in the way you should go. I am your redeemer and make right all your ways. Listen to me. Wait for me. I've waited for you. Dangers lurk on the streets of life, but with me all is safe. I will always shine a light into the darkness and expose the evil that awaits – I will keep you safe. Cling to me. Remember my presence. Lift me up in song and praise often. Keep attuned to my voice and use your hearing ear. I cry out in the streets waiting for my loved ones to tune in with listening ears. I want you to hear even my whisper … because I love you.

Scripture:

"Teach me to do your will, for you are my God; may your good Spirit lead me on level ground." (Psalm 143:10 - NIV)

"Listen, my son, accept what I say, and the years of your life will be many. I instruct you in the way of wisdom and lead you along straight paths. When you walk, your steps will not be hampered; when you run, you will not stumble. Hold on to instruction, do not let it go; guard it well, for it is your life." (Proverbs 4:10-13 - NIV)

"For we are mingled with the Messiah..." (Hebrews 3:14 - TPT)

"TRUST ME"

Lord, I give everything I hold dear to you…

His Response:

The world is dark, and full of confusion, but as you lift your loved ones to me in the atmosphere where no evil dwells, I can shine my perfect light upon them. Yes, my light is a light of healing. My burden is light. My light shines in the very darkness. My presence is made known throughout the earth. Come to me often. Bring me your children. Bring me your concerns. Trust me and entrust all to me. I am your healer. I am your counselor. I am the lover of your soul. I am your creator and your very life. Bring all that concerns you to me. My lap is the lap of love. I know how to work out the tiniest of details to perfection. Entrust everything to me and all will be well with your soul. I am the Alpha and the Omega, the director of the universe. I know the course of each life, and when entrusted to me and yielded up to me, I can do amazing things. Learn to let go often. Never hold on. When you do, you hinder my work. Trust me and entrust all to me often. I am to be trusted. I Am.

Scripture:

"Come to me, all you who are weary and burdened, and I will give you rest. Take my yoke upon you and learn from me, for I am gentle and humble in heart, and you will find rest for your souls. For my yoke is easy and my burden is light." (Matthew 11:28 – 30, NIV)

"Pour out all your worries and stress upon Him and leave them there, for He always tenderly cares for you." (1 Peter 5:7 - TPT)

"MY WAYS WILL PREVAIL"

My Question:

Lord, please speak to me about our president, our country and our future. I'm listening and need to hear from you.

His Answer:

My plans and purposes will prevail. All that men do is in vain when they are not looking to me. Walls built by men will crumble. Cities will fall and lie in ruin. Remember, I am your fortress and your strength. Look to me and all will be well with your soul. I will lead you and guide you. I will help you navigate the deep waters that lie ahead. Yes, even though the waters will be deep, look to me. I will shine my light on the paths you should go. Learn to look to me in every detail of your life – even the smallest. I am a Big God and can provide for every one of your needs. Entrust all to me. Entrust your family to me, for they are mine. I will show you where you should go. Come to me often. The days ahead are dark, but for you and all who trust in me they will be as the noonday sun. My ways will prevail.

Scripture:

"…no weapon forged against you will prevail, and you will refute every tongue that accuses you…" (Isaiah 54:17 - NIV)

"You are my strength, I sing praise to you; you, God, are my fortress, my God on whom I can rely." (Psalm 59:17 - NIV)

"LIVE IN MY LOVE"

My Question:

"Be imitators of God…" Lord, you are so patient with us, and gracious beyond measure. Tell me how we can imitate you. We want to be more like you.

His Answer:

Look to me – as your face is toward mine, my reflection will be on you.

I want you to reflect my love to all you meet. Even the downcast will be lifted up. Love is a powerful force. It heals. It delivers. It builds up. It protects. It sets free. Live in my love and give it away freely as I freely give my love to you.

Scripture:

"Be imitators of God in everything you do, for then you will represent your Father as his beloved sons and daughters. And continue to walk surrendered to the extravagant love of Christ, for he surrendered his life as a sacrifice for us…" (Ephesians 5:1, 2 – TPT)

(1 Corinthiams 13:1-13 – TPT)

"I AM YOUR BURDEN BEARER"

My Question:

"Take my yoke upon you and learn from me, for I am gentle and humble in heart, and you will find rest for your souls. For my yoke is easy, and my burden is light." (Matthew 11:29,30)

Father, thank you that you are a loving Father – one who lightens our burdens. You do not burden us with the guilt and shame that we deserve, but you are the one who lifts it from us when we come to you. Thank you. Teach us to have a gentle spirit and a humble heart like yours. Help us. Tell us about your gentle spirit and humble heart.

His Answer:

I laid my life down for you. True humility is loving so much that you are willing to lose yourself for another. Lose your dignity, as David did when he danced. Lose your pride – the very pride the Pharisees longed to hold onto as I came into their view. They hated me and despised me. I was forsaken by all men. I looked to my Father always and only said what I heard Him say. As you focus your attention on me and learn to incline your ear toward me and your spirit toward mine, you will find yourself aligned with me. You are my hands and my feet. You are to bear one another's burdens and love so much that you are compelled to go out of your comfort zone to touch others and to set them free. Only love can do this. Love compels to go out and be my hands and feet – to bring my very presence to a weary world. Yes, people are burdened down by the cares of this world. Yea, I long to lift them up, for my yoke is easy and my burden is light. As with oxen – two harnessed together are much stronger than one. One lifts the other's weight and burden, making it easy to bear. I am your burden bearer. Come to Me.

Scripture:

"Come to me, all you who are weary and burdened, and I will give you rest." (Matthew 11:28, NIV)

Jesus said "…this is my parting command: Love one another deeply!" (John 15:17, TPT)

"RESTORED AND REFRESHED"

My Question:

Lord, what are your thoughts concerning stillness?

His Answer:

I long to quiet every ache in your heart. I say be still and know that I am God – your God – the lover of your soul. Be still. Take my yoke upon you, for it is easy. I am your burden bearer. I do not want you to be burdened down by the cares of life. I came to lift them up from you. I came to lift you up to myself and make you My very own. I am the one who longs to quiet your heart like a mother quiets her infant child.

Come to me, and I will still your soul and breathe new life into you. I will restore you and refresh you as you set yourself quietly in My presence. I am like a shower, gently raining down on you my love.

Scripture:

"Are you weary, carrying a heavy burden? Then come to me. I will refresh your life, for I am your oasis. Simply join your life with mine. Learn my ways and you'll discover that I am gentle, humble, easy to please. You will find refreshment and rest in me. For all that I require of you will be pleasant and easy to bear." (Matthew 11:28-30 - TPT)

"He says, "Be still, and know that I am God; I will be exalted among the nations, I will be exalted in the earth." (Psalm 46:10 - NIV)

"I WILL LEAD YOU"

My Question:

Father, tell me about the destiny you placed in us.

His Answer:

Your destiny is in me. I in you and you in me. As you listen to me and hear my voice, I will lead you and tell you where you should go and what you should be about.

Learn to have a listening ear. Just as I did what I saw my Father do and said what I heard my Father say, I want you to do what you see me do and say what you hear me say. My Spirit is within you and will make known these things to you. Listen and see. Listen with your inner ear, and see with the eyes of your heart. This is your spirit. Yes, your spirit is growing. It is learning how to see and hear of me. Take joy, my child, as I rejoice over you with singing.

Scripture:

"What no eye has seen, what no ear has heard, and what no human mind has conceived" – the things God has prepared for those who love him- these are the things God has revealed to us by his Spirit." (1 Corinthians 2:9,10 - NIV)

"I hear the Lord saying, "I will stay close to you, instructing and guiding you along the pathway for your life. I will advise you along the way and lead you forth with my eyes as your guide." (Psalm 32:8,9 – TPT)

"The Lord your God is with you, the Mighty Warrior who saves. He will take great delight in you; in his love he will no longer rebuke you, but will rejoice over you with singing." (Zephaniah 3:17 - NIV)

"WITH ME YOU CAN DO ALL THINGS"

My Question:

Father, will you make my love increase and overflow for others? I need this more and more. I desire this. How will you do this? How does it happen?

His Answer:

I in you and you in me. By my Spirit, says the Lord. Yes, my Spirit within you takes the rough edges and makes them smooth. It is a work only I can do. You trying to love is like you trying to fly. No, but with me, you can do all things. With me you can love the unlovable. With me you can endure being crushed. With me your words can remain sweet. With me you can pray for those who have committed heinous crimes that make you want to hate.

Stay with me and let me increase in you. With me there is increase. I am the one who is able to increase my love in you. I am the only one who can do this. This is my work, and a marvelous work it is.

Scripture:

"And may the Lord increase your love until it overflows toward one another and for all people, just as our love overflows toward you." (1 Thessalonians 3:12 – TPT)

"REMEMBER ME"

My Question:

Jesus, you said "Here I am! I stand at the door and knock. If anyone hears my voice and opens the door, I will come in and eat with that person, and they with me". (Revelation 3:20 - NIV)

I open the door and am waiting to hear a word from you, Jesus. What do you want to say?

His Answer:

I am the holy one whom you adore. I am your Savior and Lord. I stand at the door and knock. I am the one who holds the key to the Kingdom. I've given you that key. You are free to enter at any time because you have my name and you are identified with me.

Your identity is in me. Remember me often. Remember me in all you do. Remembrance of me will remind you of who you are and the privileges you enjoy. Remembering me will remind you of the burdens you are to gladly bear, for I have been lifted up for all men, and I am the one who takes away the sin of the world.

Remember to yoke yourself with me. As you bear others burdens through love, you will lean on me and let me bear them for you and take them from you. You are an extension of me while you are here on this earth.

Be about my business. The time is short. Be about my business. Come to me often. Remember me.

Scripture:

"Stretch out your hand of power through us to heal, and to move in signs and wonders by the name of your holy Son, Jesus!" (Acts 4:30 – TPT)

"I AM DOING A NEW THING"

My Question:

Father, this morning I was reading about Jesus' illustration of putting a new patch on an old garment and how the patch would tear away and ruin the garment, and how you can't put new wine in old wineskins, for the wineskins would burst. New wine must be put in new wineskins. I think I received illumination on this from the Holy Spirit that this is depicting the Old Covenant vs. the New. (Matthew 9:14-17)

Will you give me more insight on this, Jesus?

His Answer:

Many of my people refuse to step into the New Covenant I provided and rent for them. They loved more what they were accustomed to. Take heed and learn from this. Never hold too tightly to the old, for I am doing a new thing – even now – in your midst.

Cling to me. Stay close and I will show you things yet to come. Yes, the time is near. I draw my bow, and the arrow is about to fly.

Stay close to me, my dear one. With me there is safety and complete joy. I will complete all things in due time. Much is yet to unfold. Like a scroll, bit by bit shall be revealed. I am the one who reveals all things.

Take heart. I love you, my child, and will show you the way in which you should go. Yeah! I am about to do a new thing. Take heed. Look for me and listen for my voice.

Scripture:

"…This cup seals the new covenant with my blood. Drink it – and whenever you drink this, do it to remember me.." (1 Corinthians 11:25 – TPT)

"See, the former things have taken place, and new things I declare; before they spring into being I announce them to you." (Isaiah 42:9 – NIV)

"THE TIME IS SHORT"

Father, thank you for the great love you have for us. You are so patient and kind.

His Response:

My patience is like a fury about to explode. My wisdom is about to be magnified and shed abroad in a disproportionate way. My glory is about to be shared with all those who love me and truly serve me. My anger is about to be tested and tasted by those who are sons of disobedience. My power is about to be displayed with magnificence and fury.

The time for patience is running short. These are the end of days. The time is short and my power is about to be displayed among the nations of the world. My word is true. Remember my word. My Holy Spirit will bring you remembrance as you need it.

Cling to me. I am life to your spirit and health to your bones. I breathe life into dry bones and refresh spirits as a stream of living water floods the deserts. I open up the very portals of Heaven for those who choose to come up here and sup with me. I am your God, the Host of Heaven, the Bright Morning Star. I linger in your very midst as you draw close to me, longing to hear from me.

Stay close. Come often. Come up. Come up here. This is my dwelling place – yes, and I shed my very presence abroad in the hearts of those who love me and are called according to my purposes.

I call you this day. Come unto me. My presence satisfies, and I long to give you the desires of your heart. I long to give you seeing eyes and a hearing ear. I long to share my Spirit nature with you. Look for me often. Come up here and sup with me, and I will give you eyes to see and ears to hear. My word is true. I am the word. I AM.

Scripture:

"Move your heart closer and closer to God, and he will come even closer to you." (James 4:8 – TPT)

"Make God the utmost delight and pleasure of your life, and he will provide for you what you desire most." (Psalm 37:4 – TPT)

"USE MY NAME AND APPLY MY BLOOD"

My Question:

Father, in Ephesians 3:10 Paul wrote "Now, through us, the manifold wisdom of God is to be made known to the rulers and authorities in the heavenly realms." Can you expand upon this? What does this mean?

His Answer:

My power is to be displayed before all rulers, powers and principalities of the evil one. I am God on High. I created all things and I will prevail over all. My kingdom will come and my will will be done on earth as it is in my holy place on high.

I will destroy the destroyer. You are to take my word and wield it against all the powers of the air. Wield my sword, which is my word. Enemy lines are cut low when you do. The enemy's plans and purposes are thwarted when you use my word. Pray often and pray much. The time is short and the enemy is fierce. My eternal purposes will prevail. Yeah, I Am that I Am that I Am. The Prince of Peace is coming, and will devour the prince of this world. With a holy fire he is coming.

Be alert and watch. The time is near. Watch and pray. Use the authority I have given in my name – the mighty name of Jesus. You will withstand the enemy with my name. You will conquer kingdoms with my name and my blood. You will reverse curses with my name and overcome all the schemes of the evil one. Use my name and apply my blood for protection. My name is powerful. My name is protection. My name is wisdom. My name is holy. My name is anointed. Apply my name in all you do.

I am the holy one who has come to save.

Scripture:

"…your kingdom come, your will be done, on earth as it is in heaven." (Matthew 6:10 – NIV)

"Take the helmet of salvation and the sword of the Spirit, which is the word of God." (Ephesians 6:17 – NIV)

"This is why you must be waiting, watching and praying, because no one knows when that season of time will come." (Mark 13:33 – TPT)

"COME TO ME FIRST"

My Question:

Lord, when I have to make important decisions in life, how can I be sure they are right?

His Answer:

When you come to me and ask, seeking my guidance in all that you do and all that you need, I am delighted. I delight to give you the desires of your heart and I delight in seeing you come to me first – before going to the world. Look to me first in all your needs. This pleases me. Trust me. Remember what you've asked of me and look for your provision from me. You will know. I will put a knowing in your spirit where you will know that you know that you know. It will be a feeling of ease. It will feel right. It will be light – like a burden lifted. You will know.

I am your God, the holy one who longs to guide your paths unto good things. I will lead you. You and me, together we will go. Stay close. Stay anointed. Come to me often for your anointing. I am your anointing. I am. Stay close.

Scripture:

"Make God the utmost delight and pleasure of your life, and he will provide for you what you desire the most." (Psalm 37:4 – TPT)

"You make known to me the path of life; you will fill me with joy in your presence, with eternal pleasures at your right hand." (Psalms 16:11 – NIV)

"May he give you the desire of your heart and make all your plans succeed." (Psalms 20:4 – NIV)

"Keep showing the humble your path, and lead them into the best decision." (Psalm 25:9 - TPT)

"LEARN TO TRUST ME MORE"

My Question:

Lord, do I have fullness of faith, hope and love concerning my loved ones?

His Answer:

You need to learn to trust me more. I am the one who gives you fullness of joy, love and peace. As you enter into my presence and still yourself, then you are able to receive from me. I am the one whom you are to entrust each one to. Entrust your loved ones to me. I am the one who knows everything about them. I know their frame. I designed them and I have purposed goodness all the days of their lives for them. I am not finished yet. Be patient and give me time. Let me be at work while you are still. My work is perfect. My work is on time. Never too early, never too late. Always on time. Trust me and see what marvelous things I have in store for you and yours as you wait upon me – your Lord.

Scripture:

Psalm 139:1-24 (A must read!)

"COME AND FIND YOUR PEACE"

My Question:

Father, what would you have to say to me today?

His Answer:

You are cleansed by the blood of my Son, Jesus, my child. You and yours are cleansed and protected. Yes, I rest my protection over each and every one of you and yours. You are my beloved. I have many purposes and plans for you.

Remain open to my word. Remain open to me. Look to me and receive. I am your radiant worship warrior. Worship me often. Enter in where I will show you great and mighty things which are to come. They may seem hazy to you now, but as time draws near, they will become more and more clear. I will reveal these things when you need to know of them. I reveal my plans as they are about to unfold. Stay close to me. Enter in to my presence often. I am the key to the Kingdom. My Kingdom is everlasting, and in it is joy and everlasting peace. Come and rest with me often and find your peace.

In this world there is revelry and discord. You must enter in with me to tune your senses and discernment. I will equip you for all you need. I am your God, and know the days ahead are dark with discord – but with me there is light!

I love you, my child. Come again. Come often. I love you.

Scripture:

"For I know the plans I have for you, declares the Lord, "plans to prosper you and not to harm you, plans to give you hope and a future." (Jeremiah 29:11 – NIV)

"Then he took a cup, and when he had given thanks, he gave it to them, saying, "Drink from it, all of you. This is my blood of the covenant, which is poured out for many for the forgiveness of sins." (Matthew 26:27,28 – NIV)

"ME IN YOU, YOU IN ME"

My Question:

Father, what would you say to me about Holiness and Sanctification?

His Answer:

Me in you and you in me. I am the one who sanctifies. I am the one who makes Holy. All you need is the desire. I delight in your desire to be Holy – I delight in your desire for further Sanctification. Only I can do this. Me in you, you in me. Together we work all things out for good to those who love me and to those who are called according to my purposes.

You love me much because I have forgiven you much. I have called you for my purposes here on this earth. I am about to reveal my purposes in a new way. The time is near and my holy purposes are about to be birthed. Take heed. Be ready. I have prepared you and called you for such a time as this.

The Holy pendulum is about to swing. The very rocks of the earth are about to be shaken. But those who put their trust in me will not be shaken. Yea, though you shall walk through the valley of the shadow of death, you will not fear. Evil will be a shadow to you and yours. I will gather you close to me and keep you safe – for my very purposes. The fouls of the air will have no place to hide, yet I will hide you and yours in my bosom.

Stay close. I love you. Stay close.

Scripture:

"And we know that in all things God works for the good of those who love him, who have been called according to his purpose." (Romans 8:28 – NIV)

"Even though I walk through the darkest valley, I will fear no evil, for you are with me…" (Psalm 23:4 – NIV)

"Because of his great love, he ordained us, so that we would be seen as holy in his eyes with an unstained innocence." (Ephesians 1:4 – TPT)

"Jesus, the Holy One, makes us holy." (Hebrews 2:11 - TPT)

"LIVE IN MY ABUNDANCE"

My Question:

Lord, what would you have to say to me today?

His Answer:

Glorify my name this day. Bring glory to me. I've created you for this very purpose – to love and come to me often. I've purposed for you to have intimate communication with me, for I know your thoughts. I know your frame. I created you and long to show you the special love I have for you.

As you come to me, I will pour out my blessing upon you – blessings of refreshment, blessings of joy, blessings of peace. I will tell you which way you should go. As you keep your eyes on me, you will not be deceived. The great deceiver is alive and well, and longs to devour my sheep. But my sheep know my voice. Listen intently to my voice and follow me. I'll show you the way you should go.

I've come to give you life. Stay close to me. Come often. I long to pour out my joy upon you – rejoice! Take joy and live in my abundance. This is my desire for you, my child, and all who are mine.

Receive and rejoice!

Scripture:

"For you created my inmost being; you knit me together in my mother's womb. I praise you because I am fearfully and wonderfully made; your works are wonderful, I know that full well. My frame was not hidden from you when I was made in the secret place…" (Psalms 139:13-15 – NIV)

"The thief comes only to steal and kill and destroy; I have come that they may have life, and have it to the full." (John 10:10 – NIV)

"My own sheep will hear my voice and I know each one, and they will follow me. I give to them the gift of eternal life and they will never be lost and no one has the power to snatch them out of my hands." (John 10:27,28 – TPT)

"EXPECT"

My Question:

Father, I am pregnant with hope and expectation this day as we meet together as the body of Christ. What should I expect to experience?

His Answer:

Expect my presence. Expect my love to pour out upon you without measure. Expect my right hand to rest upon you. Expect my blood to wash you clean. Expect my miracles to flow like a seamless river of life. Expect my holy angels to be present to watch over my work. Expect the gates of hell to try to prevail – but they will not!

Expect my people to come with much thirst and many needs. Expect great things to be accomplished on behalf of my people. Expect my love to flow freely. Expect my Spirit to be at work in and amongst you. Expect my peace to be upon you. Expect my laughter to spring up from within my weary children. Expect dancing like David danced. Expect great songs of joy and resound.

Yes, my dear one, come expecting me to be your Father – loving each one of you as if you were my only one. Your expectation thrills my heart and allows me to move freely in your midst as I will. Expect and receive. For I long to give you that which you desire – that which you need. I want to make your joy full so that you will know that I am your God. Your Father. The lover of your soul.

Come!

Scripture:

"There is a time for everything, and a season for every activity under the heavens … a time to weep and a time to laugh…" (Ecclesiastes 3:1 and 3:4 – NIV)

"Wearing a linen ephod, David was dancing before the Lord with all his might, while he and all Israel were bringing up the ark of the Lord with shouts and the sound of trumpets." (2 Samuel 6:14 – NIV)

"I LONG TO BE KNOWN"

As I was listening to a CD by Nigel Mumford and Mark Kelso playing music "in the Spirit", the Lord gave me the following words.

He Said:

Peace, be still and know that I am God. I am your God – able – well able to deliver you out of all of life's circumstances.

Come to me. I cry out for you – as a voice in the desert. I long to water your thirsty souls. Come – drink of me often – drink of me much. I have more than enough. I am your Jehovah Jirah and long to fill your cup to overflowing so that the world will see me in you. Come so you can water many other dry and thirsty souls through me. But you must be still and come to know me – really know me.

I long to be known. I long to be found. I long for your love and affection – the kind of love and affection Jesus has for me and I have for him. My Spirit will bring you in. Come. We will dance. We will spin. We will laugh. We will chat. We will sit. We will intertwine our hearts – whereby yours will find mending, refreshing and joy.

This is my delight – to give it all to you, and to watch you give it away.

Scripture:

"You must worship no other Gods, but only the Lord, for he is a God who is passionate about his relationship with you." (Exodus 33:14 – NLT)

"Eternal life means to know and experience you as the only true God, and to know and experience Jesus Christ, as the Son whom you have sent." (John 17:3 – TPT)

"MY PURPOSES WILL PREVAIL"

My Question:

Lord, what are you doing now – what are you planning?

His Answer:

This is a time of preparation. I am preparing my church, my bride. I am adorning her in radiant armor. I am setting a watch upon her feet so that she will know when the time has come to move out. I am making her hands skillful, and her lips wise. Her armor is being sharpened for battle. I'm preparing wings like the eagles to be ready to lift her up in times of need. Her feet are being shod for battle. My Word is her very sustenance. It will sustain her as she eats. My Spirit will quench her thirst. Flaming arrows will not harm her, for I have given her the garment of armor, and I have shown her the garment of praise.

My horses are getting ready for battle. My heavenly hosts are at my command. Just speak my Word and they will do my bidding. Sharpen your swords, oh my people. Bend your knees and prostrate yourselves before me. Seek my face. Seek my marching orders. I have chosen you, and am readying you to perform my miraculous signs that will draw people to me with great wonder. The times are about to shift quickly. Get ready. I want my bride ready and well able to defend my purposes – for I have purposed these things to unfold at such a time as this, and I have appointed you my children, my church, my bride. I love you with a relentless love – an unyielding love.

My purposes will prevail, and my church will be triumphant – but you must prepare yourselves for readiness. I've given you everything you need. Now, learn how to use it, and use it well. Know that I am with you always. I Am

Scripture:

"Remember the former things of long ago. I am God and there is no other. I am God and there is none like me. I make known the end from the beginning, from ancient times, what is still to come. I say: My purpose will stand, and I will do all that I please. From the east I summon a bird of prey; from a far-off land, a man to fulfill my purpose. What I have said, that will I bring about. What I have planned, that will I do." (Isaiah 46:9-11 – NIV)

"LEARN TO LISTEN MORE THAN YOU SPEAK"

My Question:

Lord, teach me – how can I yield myself more fully to you? What does that look like?

His Answer:

I delight in your desire to learn to yield to me. My child, yielding is an offering of love for me; putting yourself on hold so that I may speak freely into your life; holding back your flesh so that I may give you my instruction.

My Son is an ultimate example of what yielding means. Study and learn from him. He will instruct you. Learn to listen more than you speak. Listen with your spirit. I will breathe my very words into you and let you know when to speak. Lean on me. Lean into me. Living waters flow from me. I am the giver of life and will give life-giving instructions to you when you listen. I love to fill my children with life. Lean into me and learn of me. I will supply all your needs. I am your supply, and the supply for a needy world. Come and yield to me often. I take great delight in your desire to commune with me. Come and sit with me a while each day – as often as you wish. I love you, my child, and will never leave you nor forsake you. Come!

Scripture:

"My dearest brothers and sisters, take this to heart: Be quick to listen, but slow to speak. And be slow to become angry…" (James 1:19 – TPT)

"I will never leave you alone, never! And I will not loosen my grip on your life!" (Hebrews 13:5 – TPT)

"Jesus stood and shouted out to the crowds – 'All you thirsty ones, come to me! Come to me and drink! Believe in me so that rivers of living water will burst out from within you, flowing from your inner-most being, just like the scripture says." (John 7:37,38 – TPT)

"Now all discipline seems to be more pain than pleasure at the time, yet later it will produce a transformation of character, bringing a harvest of righteousness and peace to those who yield to it." (Hebrews 12:11 - TPT)

"I DESIRE TO DO A NEW THING"

My Question:

Lord, I know that Holy Spirit lives in us if we belong to Christ – and it is the Spirit of Christ, therefore, who dwells in us. (Romans 8:9) The mind controlled by the Spirit is life and peace. (Romans 8:6) I set my mind on what you, Holy Spirit, desire of me as well as the body of Christ at this point in time. I ask you – What is it you desire of us? What should we be about?

His Answer:

You are to be as loaves of bread – broken for me. You are to be new wine, ready to be poured out on a needy people. I have sharpened you as arrows in my quiver. You are to pierce the darkness and increase my bride. New wine and fresh bread will bring increase. I will give you instruction as you look to me and seek me daily. Stay close. Come up and sup with me often. I will show you hidden treasures and new ways of doing things. I desire to do a new thing. Come higher, come up. Taste and see my goodness. My goodness is about to be poured out on all flesh. I desire my people. My heart is for all to come unto me.

The time is short, and I must be about my Father's business. Heal the sick, teach of me, love the unlovable. Draw all men unto me. Miracles and signs and wonders draw men unto me. Love draws men to me. Many are hungering, and many are proud. I will use you to sort the wheat from the tares. People will receive me, and there will be those who scoff. Be ready. Prepare yourselves for battle and prepare yourselves for ministry so that my glory will shine forth.

I will use you, each and every one. Incline your ear to me. I am with you and I will be with you always.

Scripture:

"He reveals deep and hidden things; he knows what lies in darkness, and light dwells with him." (Daniel 2:22 – NIV)

"For our spiritual wealth is in him, like hidden treasure waiting to be discovered – heaven's wisdom and endless riches of revelation knowledge." (Colossians 2:3 – TPT)

"You must allow them both to grow together until the time of harvest. At that time, I'll tell my harvesters to make sure they gather the weeds first and tie them all in bundles to be burned. Then they will harvest the wheat and put it into my barn." (Matthew 13:30 – TPT)

"I WILL RULE AND REIGN FOREVER"

My Question:

During the 40 days after Jesus' crucifixion (Acts 1;1-3), he talked with the apostles about the Kingdom of God. Lord, what are some of the things you shared with them about "The Kingdom of God"?

His Answer:

My Kingdom is without end. I will rule and reign forever. My majesty will be made known to the nations – all the nations of the earth. My authority will never end. You, my saints and priests, will dwell there with me. You will continue to bring glory to my name. You will glorify the Father and the Son through the Spirit. By the Spirit, you will live and dwell and have your being.

The Kingdom of God is higher than your comprehension right now, but I will make it known to you in my perfect time. Remain in me, my dear one. Tend to and feed my lambs and my sheep. I have given you much. To them who have much, much is required. Be prepared. Be ready. I am about to do a new thing. I love you.

Scripture:

"Your kingdom is an everlasting kingdom, and your dominion endures through all generations." (Psalms 145:13 – NIV)

"CO-OPERATE WITH ME"

My Question:

Lord, thank you for desiring to reveal your presence to us. I desire to experience more of your presence. Help me.

His Response:

When your desire becomes my desire, I have something to work with. All I desire from my children is cooperation. I need you to co-operate with me. I knock, you open the door. You pray, I provide. You ask, I provide for the need. You and me working together, revealing my very plans and purposes to a needy world. Co-operate with me and I'll show you heights as on wings of angels. I'll take you to depths no man could imagine, revealing my secrets and hidden treasures.

I love you with a relentless love, and love being loved in the same manner – for I made you in my image. Me in you, you in me. Remain, my precious one. Remain and wait for me.

Scripture:

"Behold, I'm standing at the door, knocking. If your heart is open to hear my voice and you open the door within, I will come in to you and feast with you, and you will feast with me."(Revelation 3:19,20 – TPT)

"For since the world began, no ear has heard and no eye has seen a God like you, who works for those who wait for him!"(Isaiah 64:4 – NIV)

"RECEIVE MY LOVE AS A GIFT"

My Question:

Father, today is "Mothers' Day", but it is Father's Day, your day every day! I love you, Lord, and give you my thanks and bring you praise. I worship your holy name – Father, Son and Holy Spirit. What would you have to say to me this day?

His Answer:

I am the Alpha and Omega, the beginning and the end. Come to me often and bring the sweet perfume of your lips. Worship at my feet, for it is there that I know you love me truly. I feel your love for me as you come to me in worship and praise and thanksgiving. I receive your love. I mingle my love with yours and refill you to overflowing. This is mine to give away. Receive my love as a gift. I am gifting you with a special gift of love. This is your desire, and I am filling the desire of your heart. I am filling your very heart with my special love. Use it wisely. Use it lavishly. It will bring others great joy. It is to give away. It will be like a stream of living water flowing from the very throne of God - pure and holy.

Come to me often and receive that which I have and long to give you freely. I am about to do a new thing, and need my bride to hear. I want you to be attentive and alert, ready to hear my voice. My sheep hear my voice. They know me. Listen, love and lean on me for understanding. I long to show you much and the time is short. Come to me often, my dear one, for I will give you sustenance and strength. I will give you what you need for today and for the days ahead.

Remain in me, for I love you and long to prove my faithfulness.

Scripture:

"I am the Alpha and the Omega," says the Lord God, "who is, and who was, and who is to come, the Almighty." (Revelation 1:8 – NIV)

"My own sheep will hear my voice and I know each one, and they will follow me. I give to them the gift of eternal life and they will never be lost and no one has the power to snatch them out of my hands. (John 10:27,28 – NIV)

"SERVE"

My Question:

Lord, what do you desire of me?

His Answer:

I have placed within you new seeds – seeds of love, seeds of compassion that rival the previous seed I've sown.

I want to use you to serve the underutilized, the undervalued, the underestimated, the underserved; those under pressure, those under satan's power, those who are caught up in the underworld.

This is a desperate generation. Those who are desperate for me are being called to release the captives from desperation and separation from me.

The time is short. The time is coming soon – very soon, sooner than you think. Keep your swords sharpened by my word. Stay connected. I am coming soon and need you to fight my battle and rescue my people. I need my warriors to rise up and stand for all I stand for. I will give you strength. I will give you power. You have my authority. Use it and use it well. I will put words in your mouth when you need them, and my word will come to your ears. Listen for me and stay close.

Tell my people I am coming soon and be ready. I love you dearly and long to see my bride ready and radiant. The fields are ripe for harvest. Go and use my sickle of love to bring in my harvest, my people – all those whom I died for. For my father so loved you that he sent me. I am the message given so that those who receive me will never perish, but have eternal life. There is no greater love than this. Go and bring my people home.

I love you.

Scripture:

"For God so loved the world that he gave his one and only Son, that whoever believes in him shall not perish but have eternal life. For God did not send his Son into the world to condemn the world, but to save the world through him." (John 3:16,17 – NIV)

"…I tell you, open your eyes and look at the fields! They are ripe for harvest." (John 4:35 – NIV)

"WHAT IS WRITTEN WILL BE"

My Question:

Lord, these are days of uncertainty. We are in the "latter days", and discovering great and awesome things to come. Will you speak to me about these things? We want to know and be ready – and prepare others to be looking for your return to "catch away" your church. Would you speak to me about these things, Lord?

His Answer:

My Dear, these are great and awesome days in which you live and move and have your being. I have prepared you as an arrow drawn of my bow. You will go where I direct my hand. My right hand. My righteous hand. All things are coming to a close as an end to a story. I am the author and what is written will be. Stay close and listen for my voice. I will direct your paths and lead you as to where you should go. I have readied you for battle and will protect you as you go forth. I will be your rear guard.

Take joy, for salvation rides on wings of eagles. My great waves of salvation are rising up. Prepare ye the way of the Lord! My salvation is swift and secure. It shall go where I tell it. Many will drink from the great and mighty cup of my salvation. Drink deeply from it and show people the way to drink of it.

My timing is perfect. All time is in my hands.

Scripture:

"Even youths grow tired and weary, and young men stumble and fall; but those who hope in the Lord will renew their strength. They will soar on wings like eagles; they will run and not grow weary, they will walk and not be faint." (Isaiah 40:30,31 – NIV)

"You have made known to me the paths of life; you will fill me with joy in your presence." (Acts 2:28 – NIV)

"FREELY GIVE"

My Question:

Lord, it dawned on me this past Sunday morning how the Communion Host – the bread – represents how you gave everything you had – your own life – for us that we may have everlasting life. Giving is a part of living. Lord, what can I give?

His Answer:

Give me your time, my dear one. Spend time with me. Time is precious. Time is short. Soon we will run out of time. There will be no need for time as I call you all home to be with me. So while we have time, use it wisely. It is a commodity to bring more people into my kingdom. It is a commodity to display my miracles and greatness to those with unbelieving hearts. Put my greatness on display so that those whose hearts are stony can receive hearts of flesh.

Stay close to me. Keep your branches ever dependent upon my vine. You are the branches, I am the vine. Life is in the vine. All things flow from the Father through the vine. Come and sup on me. In me lie all my promises, power and possessions. What is mine is yours. I freely give all that is mine to you. Learn to believe and receive all that I have for you, for all that I have is yours to give away. I came to give. You are called in the very likeness of me; so freely give.

Scripture:

"I will give them an undivided heart and put a new spirit in them: I will remove from them their heart of stone and give them a heart of flesh." (Ezekiel 11:19 – NIV)

"I am the vine; you are the branches. If you remain in me and I in you, you will bear much fruit; apart from me you can do nothing." (John 15:5 – NIV)

"I WILL NOT RETURN IN VAIN"

My Question:

Lord, I was led to read Luke this morning, and my eyes fell upon Luke 10:17-24 and my spirit leapt within me! "And He turned to his disciples and said privately "Blessed are the eyes that see the things you see; for I tell you that many prophets and kings have desired to see what you see, and have not seen it, and to hear what you hear, and have not heard it."

Father, tell me more about the end of days and about what I've been seeing and hearing about the times in which we're in. What should we be doing? What's our part?

His Answer:

To whom much has been given, much is required. Inquire of me often. Stay close. Your great reward is coming soon. I will not delay. My timing is perfect and I am always on time, for my plans and purposes will prevail. I am holy, and I am coming to receive my holy bride.

Continue to teach and warn my people of my impending coming. Just as my word does not return void, I will not return in vain. I want all to be in my reception – I want to receive my full house. I want all who are mine to be in my house. In me there is safety. Use the authority I have given you in my name. I will be your defense. Come to me often. Remain in me and inquire of me. I will lead you in the way you should go. My heavenly hosts are at your command. Speak my word and they will go and defend my people. Use the authority I have given you well, and all will be well with you.

Stay close and remain in me!

Scripture:

"Seek the Lord while he may be found; call on him while he is near. Let the wicked forsake their ways and the unrighteous their thoughts. Let them turn to the Lord, and he will have mercy on them, and to our God, for he will freely pardon." (Isaiah 55; 6,7 – NIV)

"Jesus replied, "While you were ministering, I watched Satan topple until he fell suddenly from heaven like lightning to the ground. Now you understand that I have imparted to you all my authority to trample over his kingdom. You will trample upon every demon before you and overcome every power satan possesses. Absolutely nothing will be able to harm you as you walk in this authority." (Luke 10:18,19 – TPT)

"PRAY UNCEASINGLY AND REMAIN IN ME"

My Question:

From things we've been seeing and learning about, this might be a significant year. Will you tell me more?

His Answer:

I am coming soon. I will not delay. Many have been awaiting the day of my return to receive my bride. The threshing floors are ready to receive their harvest. The sickle is ready to strike. Many will be amazed at my coming. Many will be caught unaware - too involved in their day-to-day business. Many listen but do not hear. I long to speak to my people – people who have a hearing ear. Most do not desire to hear from me. They seek counsel in other things. I am the great counselor. Come to me and I will show you great and mighty things to come. Seas of people will be caught unaware.

You are my voice – use it. You are my hands, use them. You are my feet, let them be tireless. They will not tire when used for my purposes. Pick up your writing utensil and write. I will give you skill. Build a wall of love around all you know, and those I will bring to you. Pray often.

Prayers of the saints are powerful and effectual. They never return void. They are a sweet aroma – rising to the Throne Room of my grace and very presence. They hold pregnant words readying themselves to burst forth into heavenly fruit – the very answers to your prayers. Fruit of your desires; Fruit of your hope; Fruit of your life in me.

Pray unceasingly and remain in me. Come to me often and I will show you great and mighty things to come. I love you. Remain in my love!

Scripture:

"As the rain and the snow come down from heaven, and do not return to it without watering the earth and making it bud and flourish, so that it yields seed for the sower and bread for the eater, so is my word that goes out from my mouth: It will not return to me empty, but will accomplish what I desire and achieve the purpose for which I sent it." (Isaiah 55: 10,11 – NIV)

"Swing the sickle, for the harvest is ripe." (Joel 3:13 – NIV)

"Pray passionately in the Spirit, as you constantly intercede with every form of prayer at all times." (Ephesians 6:18 – TPT)

"PUT ME ON DISPLAY"

My Question:

Lord, in Psalm 45:1 you said "My heart is overflowing with a good theme; I recite my composition concerning the king; my tongue is the pen of a skillful writer…"

Lord, you've given me "skill of writing" by worshipping you and stilling myself in your presence and desiring to hear from you – and then writing what I hear the Holy Spirit shares with me. This is too glorious for me to comprehend. What should I do with this?

His Answer:

Remember the one in the word with the one talent who buried it, fearing I was a harsh God? Yet the one who had five and doubled it doubled my joy in this same way by giving it away.

Put me on display. Shout it from the rooftops. Publish my glorious acts. I came to display my story to a fallen world. Use your talent and commune with me often. I will give you fresh bread – a fresh word from heaven to lead you in the way you should go. These are the days in which you must stay close. Cling to me and I will lead you. I will show you the desires of my heart. I have given you an open door to come as you wish. I am your loving father. Whatever you ask of me, I will answer, for I love you. Inquire of me. Put me to the test. My desire is to turn no one away. Come to me all who are weary, and I will give you rest. Come to me if you desire to know the secrets of my kingdom, and I will show you great and mighty things. Do not be afraid. My inquisitive children bring me great joy! I take great joy in communing with you, my children, for this is why you were created. I desire the intimacy of relationship with each one of my children. I want my sons and daughters to be desirous of me. Come, knock; my door is open. You are knocking on an open door.

Come often, come freely. You make my joy full when you come.

Scripture:

"He said to me, "You are my servant, Israel, in whom I will display my splendor." (Isaiah 49:3 –NIV)

"Ask and it will be given to you; seek and you will find; knock and the door will be opened to you. For everyone who asks receives; the one who seeks finds; and to the one who knocks, the door will be opened. (Matthew 7:7,8 – NIV)

"COME AND LEAN ON ME"

My Question:

What would you have to say to me today, Lord?

His Answer:

I want you to come and lean on me. Come and lean for a while. Draw your strength from me. I am the vine, you are the branches. You can do no good thing apart from me. I long to give you my hope and my strength. My love is an everlasting love for you. From everlasting to everlasting my love is a signal of my promise, for my promise to you is everlasting life. Yes, to all who are mine, these promises are yea and amen!

Fear not. Come to me often, for in me is life. Draw your strength from me – not from the things of this world! You are not of this world, but citizens of my kingdom. You are kings and priests of the Most High. Come up here – I want you to take in my heavenly perspective. Earthly things are diminished from my perspective. My plans and purposes will prevail despite what you see from earth's perspective.

Violence swallows up the news, but the good news is that the kingdom of God suffers violence, but the violent take it by force. I've designed my people to be violent lovers, for my love is a violent love - pure, holy and strong. I've designed my people to be violent prayers. So come up here and make your requests known to me, for I am your Holy Father. I have all that you need. Ask and you shall receive.

Come close and sup with me often. Cling to me. I am your strength, the lover of your soul. I will keep you in all your ways and fulfill all my promises.

I am trustworthy and true.

Scripture:

"I am the vine; you are the branches. If you remain in me and I in you, you will bear much fruit; apart from me you can do nothing." (John 15:5 – NIV)

"So you are not foreigners or guests, but rather you are the children of the city of the holy ones, with all the rights as family members of the household of God."(Ephesians 2:19 – TPT)

"From the moment John stepped onto the scene until now, the realm of heaven's kingdom is bursting forth and passionate people have taken hold of its power." (Matthew 11:12 – TPT)

"THE MORE YOU SPEND TIME WITH ME, THE MORE YOU WILL LOOK LIKE ME"

My Question:

Lord, what do you want to say to me right now?

His Answer:

I love when you come into my presence. I created you for communion with me. My heart delights when you come. All eternity awaits. We will have eternal time together. I want you to learn of my love for you – how I adore you and created you in my Father's very image.

The more you spend time with me, the more you will look like me. The more you spend time with me, the more you will love like me. Come to me often. I long to impart myself to you. I delight in your presence. As you learn to love me more deeply, the more I can impart my spirit upon you. Your love for me makes more room for Holy Spirit to impart his work within you.

Rest in me dear one, and know that I delight in you!

Scripture:

"Then God said, 'Let us make mankind in our image, in our likeness, so that they may rule over the fish in the sea and the birds in the sky, over the livestock and all the wild animals, and over all the creatures that move along the ground.' So God created mankind in his own image, in the image of God he created them; male and female he created them." (Genesis 1:26,27 – NIV)

"… for in the image of God has God made mankind." (Genesis 9:6 – NIV)

"Be imitators of God in everything you do, for then you will represent your Father as his beloved sons and daughters." (Ephesians 5:1 – TPT)

"For he knew all about us before we were born and he destined us from the beginning to share the likeness of his Son." (Ephesians 8:29 – TPT)

"I AM WITH YOU ALWAYS"

My Question:

Lord, where would you like to meet with me today?

His Answer:

I am with you always. Come and meet with me early in the morning. I will give life to your spirit. Come sup with me daily. Never forget I am with you. Whatever you ask I will answer. My courts are open for you to come. I long to lavish my love upon you as a sweet smelling aroma. Mingle your prayers with my purposes. From the beginning of time my purposes have been established and will prevail.

I need my people to open the veil to my purposes and pull them down. My purposes are trustworthy and true. They bring divine righteousness and everlasting life. They bring justice and mercy, yet to some - indignation and contempt. They prove the righteous and disqualify the scoffers – those who gnash their teeth at me.

Come all ye righteous and sit at my feet. Enter into open courts and come. I have appointed times with you. Special times with you. Special times for each of you – for each of you are special to me. Open your ears and eyes and I will fill them with things you have not yet seen or heard. Lift up your hearts so that I may fill them with good things. My very breath will cleanse them and renew them and revive them.

Do not be discouraged. Take heart. Take my heart. I in you and you in me. Together we will go and my purposes will be fulfilled. I love you as my very own children.

Stay close. I love you.

Scripture:

"We have become the unmistakable aroma of the victory of the Anointed One to God – a perfume of life to those being saved and the odor of death to those who are perishing. The unbelievers smell a deadly stench that leads to death, but believers smell the life-giving aroma that leads to abundant life." (2 Corinthians 2:15,16 – TPT)

"You anoint me with the fragrance of your Holy Spirit..." (Psalm 23:5 - TPT)

"A GIFT IS NOT A GIFT UNTIL IT'S GIVEN AWAY"

My Question:

Lord, what gift would you like to give me today?

His Answer:

I have given you the gift of life. Your life is a gift from me. You are my gift to those around you. Use it well. Bless those who come in contact with you. Let kindness and love pour out onto a needy world. Lay your hands on the sick of body, mind and spirit that they may be made whole.

I came to give life and am pouring it out through you, my vessels. Heap prayers upon prayers. Layers of prayers penetrate my glory and get my attention. Not one falls to the ground. I take each one and manifest my glory in them. My Heavenly Hosts are assigned to each one. I am the King of Kings and Lord of Lords. My gift I brought to you. Now bring me your gifts, for a gift is not a gift until it is given away. Give yourselves away to the poor and needy. There are many who are poor in spirit and need a touch from the Master's hand. Extend my hand to the nations and to all those in need, for in my hand there is healing. In my hand there is power. In my name, extend my hand, for in my hand is my love.

And remember, there is nothing that can separate you from my love!

Scripture:

"I tell you this timeless truth: The person who follows me in faith, believing in me, will do the same mighty miracles that I do – even greater miracles than these because I go to be with my Father! For I will do whatever you ask me to do when you ask me in my name." (John 14:12,13 – TPT)

"…I have come that they may have life, and have it to the full." (John 10:10 – NIV)

"For I am convinced that neither death nor life, neither angels nor demons, neither the present nor the future, nor any powers, neither height nor depth, nor anything else in all creation, will be able to separate us from the love of God that is in Christ Jesus our Lord." (Romans 8:39 – NIV)

"YOU ARE MY HANDS, FEET AND VOICE"

My Question:

Lord, I want to be wise and make the most of every opportunity, for time is short, and the days in which we live are evil. We are coming into desperate times, as Ephesians 5 speaks of. Jesus, share with me your heart on this matter, please. How can we serve you and others in these coming days?

His Answer:

I desire the prayers of my saints. Just as my word that goes out from my mouth does not return void, my word that goes out from your mouth never returns void, but will accomplish the purposes for which I send it. You, my children, are my very hands, feet and voice. Stay close and learn from me. The days are dark, but I am the light of the world and will shine my light forth from you.

You are like watchmen on the wall. I will give you what you need in due time. As you need it, my supply will be there for you. One day at a time. Your hearts will not grow faint. Lean on me. Soar with me. Just as the eagle has keen sight, I will give you eyes to see as time draws near. For now, I will give my provision one day at a time.

Stay close, my children. Stay close, lean on me, and pray.

Scripture:

"As the rain and the snow come down from heaven, and do not return to it without watering the earth and making it bud and flourish, so that it yields seed for the sower and bread for the eater, so is my word that goes out from my mouth: It will not return to me empty, but will accomplish what I desire and achieve the purpose for which I sent it."(Isaiah 55:10,11 – NIV)

"Son of man, I have made you a watchman for the people of Israel…" (Ezekiel 3:17 – NIV)

"BE NOT AFRAID"

My Question:

It has been a while Lord since I've journaled with you. What would you have to say to me today?

His Answer:

I have put my very Spirit in you and you are to follow Him closely. I have given you a hearing ear and eyes to see. You will see my very plans and purposes unfold before your eyes. The time is nye. Nearer than you think. Prepare ye the way, for I am coming soon. I will not delay. My timing is perfect and was set from the very beginning of time.

Do not fear, though the days ahead look dark, I am the light of the world and will overcome. You are to be a people who overcome, for you are mine and are to put me on display for all the earth to see. Put on my garments and wear them well. I will do my work through you. Be prepared. Be ready, for I am coming soon.

Be not afraid, for I will hold you close. There is no shadow of turning with me.

Scripture:

"Every gift God freely gives us is good and perfect, streaming down from the Father of lights, who shines from the heavens with no hidden shadow or darkness and is never subject to change." (James 1:17 – TPT)

James 1:17 (Footnote in The Passion Translation)

There is nothing that you will find wrong with God, nothing in Him that could even remotely appear to be evil hiding. The more you get to know Him, the more you realize how beautiful and holy he is.

"I LOVE TO SHARE MY SECRETS WITH YOU"

My Question:

Father, I delight in your presence. What would you have to say to me today?

His Answer:

I take delight in you coming to me and spending time with me. You are a sweet aroma. When you come in the name of my Son who you love, I take great delight, for He is the object of my love.

The oracles of old were confounded – the wise were perplexed, but you have found wisdom and have chosen rightly, for you know my Son. Keep seeking Him and His wisdom. Seek my Spirit often and you will find your feet on the right path. My power will go forth from your hands as you rightly seek me. Do what my Son did – stay close to me and inquire of me often. My Spirit will go where I send him. He is wisdom. He is power. He is beauty. He is strength. Rely on Him. Invite Him in often to all your circumstances. He freely gives. He is the giver of freedom and life.

Remain in me and I will remain in you. Choose wisely, and remember I am with you always, and am here to help in time of need. Call on me. I am yours. My very signature has sealed you for the day of redemption. I love your childlike presence – a sweet aroma unto me.

Come often. Come much. Inquire of me and I will answer. I am the Ancient of Days and all answers remain in me. And remember, I love to share my secrets with you – my hidden treasures, for you are the one I treasure.

Scripture:

"Call to me and I will answer you and tell you great and unsearchable things you do not know." (Jeremiah 33:3 – NIV)

"Remain in me, as I also remain in you…" (John 15:4 – NIV)

"And do not grieve the Holy Spirit of God, with whom you were sealed for the day of redemption." (Ephesians 4:30 – NIV)

"USE YOUR GIFTS AND USE THEM WELL"

To all who want to be used by the Lord:

He said:

I have given you all great skill and timely treasures. Share the treasures I have given, and will continue to give with others, for they are universal. Put Me on display. Put My words on display for all to see, for I long to speak life into all those who will hear.

I will give listening eyes and seeing ears. I will help you navigate the days ahead, for I am the great navigator – your Creator God! Use your gifts and use them well for my kingdom. I want my people ready. I want my people prepared. I want my people to be hungry for Me. I want my people to come and drink from my living water. I want my people to be warned.

Scripture:

"…I have come to give you everything in abundance, more than you expect – life in its fullness until you overflow!" (John 10:10 – TPT)

(I questioned the Lord about listening eyes and seeing ears, and he shared with me that we can perceive through our eyes and ears more than they see and hear.)

"ALL MY CREATION IS IN GOOD KEEPING WITH ME"

My Question:

We had to give our dog, Charlie Brown back to God this day. We are grateful, as many of you are, for the amazing gift our pets are to us. I asked "God, will you come and comfort me?"

His Answer:

I am the lover of your soul and your strength and comforter. All I have is yours, and all you have is in good keeping with me. All my creation is in good keeping with me. I lose not one. All are mine and will be safe. I will shepherd your heart. Lean not on your own understanding. Seek me often. I am here to be found. You have found me, and I delight in you. I will quench your thirst and fill your life with good things. All good things come from me. Look to me often and rest in my love.

Scripture:

"…the creation itself will be liberated from its bondage to decay and brought into the freedom and glory of the children of God." (Romans 8:20,21 – NIV)

"…with eager expectation, all creation longs for freedom from its slavery to decay and to experience with us the wonderful freedom coming to God's children." (Romans 8:20,2l – TPT)

"I'LL NEVER LEAVE YOU NOR LET GO OF YOU"

A Message From the Lord:

To My dear dear children:

I love you with a love that is higher than your comprehension - love that is unquenchable and will never die. I will never leave you nor forsake you. I will stick close by your side – closer than a brother or sister.

I came for you, and have many plans for you. Stay close to me. I will unfold the plans for your future, one step at a time. Be reliant on me, for I am your true joy giver. All good things flow from me. Be patient. Turn to me. I love you and will never leave you nor let go of you. When you are frightened or feel alone, come to me and I will comfort you. I am your Heavenly Father who knows your frame and loved you as you were being formed in your mother's womb. Even before you were conceived, I knew you and loved you. Come, and stay close to me. I will shelter you and be your provider all the days of your life. I long to give you good gifts – a future filled with joy and hope. I long to give you the desires of your heart.

Stay close and know that I love you, and always will.

Your Heavenly Father, I AM

Scripture:

"I will never leave you nor forsake you." (Joshua 1:5 – NIV)

"For I know the plans I have for you, declares the Lord, Plans to prosper you and not to harm you, plans to give you hope and a future." (Jeremiah 29:11 – NIV)

"Let joy overflow, for you are united with the Anointed One!" (Philippians 4:4 – TPT)

"For you created my inmost being. You knit me together in my mother's womb." (Psalm 139:13 – NIV)

"Take delight in the Lord, and he will give you the desires of your heart." (Psalm 37:4 – NIV)

"I HAVE APPOINTED YOU FOR SUCH A TIME AS THIS"

My Question:

Father, Jesus said "Whoever belongs to God hears what God says". (John 8:47) What would you have to say to me today?

His Answer:

"Hold tight to me and my word. Many things are about to unfold. Things that will perplex the world and even confound the wise. I am wisdom. Stay close. I have appointed you for such a time as this. Be ready when I speak. Let nothing hinder you. There will be wars and rumors of wars. Everything that can shake will be shaken, but all who are in me will not be shaken. I want you to know the times in which you are living. Yes, they are dangerous times, yet my plans will prevail. I am a jealous God, an all-consuming fire. My plans will prevail.

You are my warriors – my mighty warriors with a voice. Just as shouts were heard in the Jericho march and the walls came down, I want you to use your voices. Voices of praise. Voices of prayer. Voices of authority. Remember I have given you authority over all the enemy. Pray for my kingdom to come and that my will may be done on earth as it is in heaven. In the days ahead, you will need ears to hear and eyes to see. Stay close and learn to hear my voice more and more each day. You are in training as a mighty warrior. Sharpen your senses and be quick to hear my voice.

I love you with an unending love and will never leave you. I am with you always – till the ends of the earth. I will never let go of you.

Your loving Father, "I Am"

Scripture:

"…And who knows but that you have come to your royal position for such a time as this?" (Esther 4:14 – NIV)

"You will hear of wars and rumors of wars, but see to it that you are not alarmed. Such things must happen, but the end is still to come. Nation will rise against nation, and kingdom against kingdom. There will be famines and earthquakes in various places. All these are the beginning of birth pains." (Matthew 24: 6-8 – NIV)

"Faith pulled down Jericho's walls after the people marched around them for seven days!" (Hebrews 11:30 – TPT)

"DRINK DEEP AND POUR"

My Question:

Jesus said…"Whoever serves me must follow me; and where I am, my servant also will be. My Father will honor the one who serves me."

Lord Jesus, how may we serve you more?

His Answer:

I want you to come and know me more. I want you to do as I did. Always look to the Father. Stay sensitive to him. And stay sensitive to Holy Spirit, who will guide you. Remain in me and I will remain in you. My Kingdom is about to come to earth and my will will be done. Keep on praying. Keep on loving. Keep on forgiving. Let my righteousness clothe you. Remember that you are clothed in me – in my righteousness. Remain conscious of this very fact. You can do nothing apart from me. My very power dwells within all who are mine.

A time is coming when I will unleash that power within you. You are my body; my feet; my hands; my mouthpiece. A time is coming soon when I will unleash my power and it will flow through you to accomplish the purposes which I have planned from the very beginning of time.

Come into the river with me. Get over your head with me. This is where you will learn to rely on me and not your own. Come and be overwhelmed by my love. Step on in. Come closer. I will hold you and never let you go. You can depend on me. My power will not harm you. Just let it flow. It is the flow of my love coursing through you. My love is my power. Take hold of it and run the race to win!

I am coming soon. Meanwhile, consume yourselves with my love, and pour it back out on those who are in need of a deep drink; those who are hungry and thirsty for me. Yes, drink deeply of me and pour me out – just as I poured myself out in a weary land. It was my Father's will to pour out my love for you, and it is his will that you continue pouring out my love until I come again.

So, drink deeply of me, my child. Drink deep and pour.

Scripture:

"…your kingdom come, your will be done, on earth as it is in heaven…" (Matthew 6:10 – NIV)

"Remain in me, as I also remain in you. No branch can bear fruit by itself; it must remain in the vine. Neither can you bear fruit unless you remain in me." (John 15:4 – NIV)

"This righteousness is given through faith in Jesus Christ to all who believe…" (Romans 3:22 – NIV)

"HE IS COMING SOON"

My Question:

1 John 16:12-15 "…He (Holy Spirit) will not speak on his own, he will only speak what he hears, and he will tell you what is yet to come…"

What is it that is yet to come, Lord?

His Answer:

Oh my child, that you would ask a question such as this. It pleases me that you come and ask, inquiring of me.

I am high, holy and lifted up. I am the King of all nations, and all nations will soon bow their knees before me.

I purposed the world into existence, and my plans are perfect. Take delight in me, as I delight in you. Stay close. Come boldly before me and ask, search, dig. I delight in your inquiring mind and spirit. I delight in your child-likeness, your trust in me. Your trust for me to answer you. To protect you and all who are yours and mine. I will tell you, a day is coming when the Prince of Peace will rule again in Jerusalem. It is coming soon. He is coming soon.

Be prepared and stay closely connected to the vine. There your fruit will grow and gush – fruit that will feed the hungry and quench those who thirst after me. Fruit that will open blind eyes, and ears that have been deaf. Fruit that will give understanding to those who need to know my love – the great love that I have for them. There is no greater love.

Remain in my love. This is where you become strengthened – in me. This is where you become nourished – in me. Remain in my love. And remember – love is the greatest of all.

"I Am" Love

Scripture:

"I love each of you with the same love that the Father loves me. You must continually let my love nourish your hearts. If you keep my commands, you will live in my love, just as I have kept my Father's commands, for I continually live nourished and empowered by his love." (John 15:9,10 – TPT)

"But the fruit produced by the Holy Spirit within you is divine love in all its varied expressions: peace that subdues, patience that endures, kindness in action, a life full of virtue, faith that prevails, gentleness of heart, and strength of spirit…" (Galatians 5:22,23 – TPT)

"THIS IS TRUE INTIMACY"

My Question:

I was reading Galatians 4:6 (the Message version) that reads "Doesn't that privilege of intimate conversation with God make it plain that you are not a slave, but a child? And if you are a child, you're also an heir, with complete access to the inheritance."

Q. What would you say about this, Father?

His Answer:

I've given you complete access to myself through my son. Through him I have received many sons and daughters. You are my great delight. I long for more children. Oh, how I long to converse with each one. I created you for conversation, for fellowship, for love. Love is not fully expressed without a receiver. Love is complete when it is given and then received. You are a receiver of my love, and I take great delight in receiving your love. This is true intimacy.

My kingdom is a kingdom of love and fellowship. Giving and receiving. It has no end. My kingdom is coming to earth soon. I will establish it in my perfect timing. Meantime, watch and be ready. I will give you signs of my coming. Have eyes to see and ears that hear. My Spirit will open your eyes and ears so that you will be sensitive to my heavenly dimension. This is my domain where I dwell. It is a high and holy place with many distant lands. One day you will see and rejoice…"As it is written:"What no eye has seen, what no ear has heard, and what no human mind has conceived" - the things God has prepared for those who love him – these are the things God has revealed to us by his Spirit." (1Cor. 2:9,10 – NIV)

So wait and you will see. Yes, my daughter, you will see.

Love, I Am – I am love

Scripture:

"He (Jesus) told them this parable: "Look at the fig tree and all the trees. When they sprout leaves, you can see for yourselves and know that summer is near. Even so, when you see these things happening, you know that the kingdom of God is near." (Luke 21:29-31 – NIV)

"I HAVE THE GIFT OF ABUNDANT LIFE FOR YOU"

My Question:

Lord, in your presence, what gift do you have for me today?

His Answer:

I have the gift of my very presence.

In my presence is life – life abundant. I have the gift of abundant life for you. It is a gift that always satisfies and never runs out. It is everlasting and more than enough. It never dries up. Never gets old. It's always alive – teaming with life. It's creative and life-inspiring. It instructs and is full of wisdom.

My gift and desire for you is the abundant life – my abundant life in you. Fill up on me each day and you will always have what you need – more than enough. Fill yourself with my love. Take it in so that you can give it away in abundant portions. My abundance overflows – come often and be filled to overflowing in my presence!

Scripture:

"The thief comes only to steal and kill and destroy; I have come that they may have life, and have it to the full." (John 10:10 – NIV)

"A thief has only one thing in mind – he wants to steal, slaughter, and destroy. But I have come to give you everything in abundance, more than you expect – life in its fullness until you overflow!" (John 10:10 – TPT)

"KNOW THAT I AM WITH YOU ALWAYS"

My Question:

Lord, I want to be pleasing to you. How may I please you more? How may I be pleasing to you, Lord?

His Answer:

Remember me. Be mindful of me. Bind yourself to me. Know that I am with you always. I've told you I will never leave you nor forsake you. Cling to my word. I am the word – the living word. Fashion your life after me. Look to me. Do what I do and say what I say.

I am a stream of living water and will quench the very thirst within you. I Am. Come to me and I will give you rest - rest for your weary soul - rest from a weary world.

Come up here, for this is where your life is – hidden in me. I want you to take my heavenly perspective. The greater one lives within you.

Remember me.

I Am

Scripture:

"…the One who is living in you is far greater than the one who is in the world." (1 John 4:4 – TPT)

"Don't be obsessed with money but live content with what you have, for you always have God's presence. For hasn't he promised you, "I will never leave you alone, never! And I will not loosen my grip on your life!" (Hebrews 13:5 – TPT)

"Are you weary, carrying a heavy burden? Then come to me. I will refresh your life, for I am your oasis. Simply join your life with mine. Learn my ways and you'll discover that I'm gentle, humble, easy to please. You will find refreshment and rest in me. For all that I require of you will be pleasant and easy to bear." (Matthew 11:28 – TPT)

"EXTEND MY LOVE TO THOSE WHO HAVE NOT YET FOUND ME"

My Question:

Give me your heavenly perspective, Lord.

His Answer:

I dwell in the most high and holy place surrounded by heavenly hosts. I am coming soon and want my bride to be ready for my coming. I've been waiting many days. A thousand years is as a day with me. I have waited patiently. My love has been patient. I long for my house to be full. I long for my house to be complete, as in the completion of days which is yet to come.

Come up here for strength. Come up here to discover your divine purposes for the day. I have divine purposes for you – for all my bride. My body is about to move out in full array – strengthened and unified in love. You will be a powerful force on the face of the earth. My kingdom is coming and my will will be done on earth as it is here in heaven.

Just as the Father is seen in the Son, the earth will display the very image of my high and holy dwelling place. It is yet to come. Be patient as I am patient, and extend my love to those who have not yet found me or received my invitation to come.

I am coming soon, but in the meantime, I want many more to come unto me. I did not come to condemn the world, but to save it.

I love you and commission you to go and be about my Father's work – until I come again.

I am waiting. I am love. I Am

Scripture:

"A thousand years in your sight are like a day that has just gone by, or like a watch in the night." (Psalms 90:4 – NIV)

"You didn't choose me, but I've chosen and commissioned you to go into the world to bear fruit." (John 15:16 – TPT) The Footnote for this verse reads: The Aramaic is "I have invited you" (as dinner guests).

"God did not send his Son into the world to judge and condemn the world, but to be its Savior and rescue it!" (John 3:17 – TPT)

"LET GO AND LIVE"

My Question:

What do you want me to give to you, Lord?

His Answer:

Whatever you are holding on to, let it go. Give everything to me – give it all.

When you release your greatest fears to me, it is like a sweet aroma. When you give me each loved one, yes, family and friends – you are giving me your offerings. These are precious offerings given unto me, for they show your trust in me – the one who is trustworthy.

I am worthy of your trust. I am worthy. I am able. I am. Give it all to me and watch me work. I am your healer. I am your enabler. I am your justification. I am your defender. I am your countenance and your very life-giver. So give it all to me and live. Yes, let go and live, for I Am!

Scripture:

"You will never worry about an attack of demonic forces nor have to fear a spirit of darkness coming against you. Don't fear a thing!" (Psalm 91:5,6 – TPT)

"All God accomplishes is flawless, faithful, and fair, and his every word proves trustworthy and true." (Psalm 111:7 – TPT)

"PEACE AND JOY UNSPEAKABLE"

My Question:

I was reading Psalm 91 (The Passion Translation). The last sentence says "For you will enjoy the fullness of My salvation". What does the fullness of your salvation look like?

His Answer:

The fullness of my salvation is peace and joy unspeakable. It is my army angels surrounding you wherever you and your loved ones go. It is strength – my strength in the midst of difficulties. It is victory in the midst of defeat. It is knowing me and my word. It is fully trusting me and trusting that I have a good outcome for you every time because I love you.

It is beauty for ashes. It is my light in place of darkness. The fullness of my salvation is my very design for you.

Come – step into it and live. It is yours for the asking. I fashioned it for you!

Scripture:

"Restore to me the joy of your salvation and grant me a willing spirit, to sustain me." (Psalm 51:12 – NIV)

"God sends angels with special orders to protect you wherever you go, defending you from all harm." (Psalm 91:11 – TPT)

"The Spirit of the Sovereign Lord is on me, because the Lord has anointed me to proclaim good news to the poor. He has sent me to bind up the brokenhearted, to proclaim freedom for the captives and release from darkness for the prisoners, to proclaim the year of the Lord's favor and the day of vengeance of our God, to comfort all who mourn, and provide for those who grieve in Zion – to bestow on them a crown of beauty instead of ashes, the oil of joy instead of mourning, and a garment of praise instead of a spirit of despair. They will be called oaks of righteousness, a planting of the Lord for the display of his splendor." (Isaiah 61:1-3 – NIV)

"YOU ARE THE OBJECT OF MY AFFECTION"

My Question:

What do you have to say to me today, Lord? I'm leaning in to hear what you have to say to me.

His Answer:

I am high and lifted up. I am your redeemer. You are the object of my affection. No harm will come to you. Do not fear. I will redeem your life and make all things new. Follow me. Follow my Spirit. He will lead you and be your guide. He will keep you safe.

I will increase your senses and discernment as you need. I am with you. Put your pen to paper. Cry out in the streets. Bring my people in – those who do not yet know me. They are mine. You are my workers. I've placed my very gifts in each of you to use for my glory and to glorify my Father. My Father is your Father.

Come and glorify us by putting your gifts to work. Each one of you is precious to me. I anoint you to go and do my work. Remember…I am meek and lowly of heart.

I Am

Scripture:

"Even though I walk through the darkest valley, I will fear no evil, for you are with me; your rod and your staff, they comfort me." (Psalms 23:4 – NIV)

"My heart is stirred by a noble theme as I recite my verses for the king; my tongue is the pen of a skillful writer." (Psalms 45:1 – NIV)

"Do you know of any parent who would give his hungry child, who asked for food, a plate of rocks instead? Or when asked for a piece of fish, what parent would offer his child a snake instead? If you, imperfect as you are, know how to lovingly take care of your children and give them what's best, how much more ready is your heavenly Father to give wonderful gifts to those who ask him?" (Matthew 7:9-11 – TPT)

"And when God chooses someone and graciously imparts gifts to him, they are never rescinded." (Romans 11:29 – TPT)

"YOU ARE ON THE VERGE OF BREAKTHROUGH"

My Question:

Father, what do you have to say to me this morning?

His Answer:

I delight in your love for one another. I delight in your love for me – your heavenly Father, my Son and my Spirit.

Remain open. Open to my Spirit. Keep your eyes and ears open to receive what I want you to know. I want you to perceive. You are my beautiful warriors. You are on the verge of breakthrough. Your prayers are breaking down enemy camps. Remain faithful in your prayer lives.

Be alert and sharpen your senses. I want you to perceive the future. I want you to know the times in which you live. No weapon formed against you will prosper. I am the Alpha and the Omega. I am your great defender. I am with you always. You are mine, and I take great delight in you.

Remain in me. I love you.

I Am

Scripture:

"...you perceive my thoughts from afar." (Psalm 139:2 – NIV)

"…no weapon forged against you will prevail…" (Isaiah 54:17 – NIV)

"…And pray in the Spirit on all occasions with all kinds of prayers and requests. With this in mind, be alert and always keep on praying for all the Lord's people." (Ephesians 6:18 – NIV)

"I AM BRINGING YOU CLOSER TO YOUR DESTINY"

My Question:

Lord, where are you taking us?

His Answer:

I am taking you on a journey of ascension. I long for you to come closer to me – to hear the beat of my heart just as my disciple John, whom I love, leaned his head upon my heart. I am taking you on a journey of greater intimacy with me, your Savior and King.

I want you to continue to press into me. I have so much to show you, and long for you to find my secret hidden treasures.

As you hear about wars and rumors of wars, do not fear. Come up here and find refuge and rest for your tender souls. I am the great navigator, and have all things in my charge. I am never too soon or too late.

Be watchful and faithful in prayer. I remind you of my word "It is the Lord who directs your life, for each step you take is ordained by God to bring you closer to your destiny". This is where I am taking you – I am bringing you closer to your destiny. Cling to me, for I Am.

Scripture:

"You will hear of wars nearby and revolutions on every side, with more rumors of wars to come. Don't panic or give in to your fears, for the breaking apart of the world's systems is destined to happen. But it won't yet be the end; it will still be unfolding." (Matthew 24:6 – TPT)

"It is the Lord who directs your life, for each step you take is ordained by God to bring you closer to your destiny. So much of your life, then remains a mystery!" (Proverbs 10:24 – TPT)

"YOU ARE NOT OF THIS WORLD"

My Question:

Lord, how may we enter deeper into your Kingdom Realm? The realm of your kingdom?

His Answer:

I have not given you a spirit of fear, but of power, love and a sound mind. Fear is of this world. You must remember – you are not of this world. Your position and authority are seated in and with me.

You must come up here often. Remind yourselves of your true dwelling place – my kingdom. My kingdom is a place filled with justice and peace. Nothing will harm you as you dwell in my midst. No fear will overtake you. Fear cannot dwell here. Sickness cannot dwell here. Hatred and unforgiveness cannot dwell here. You are not of this world. You are of my kingdom. You must constantly be reminded of such. This is how you will live victoriously – with me.

Apart from me you can do nothing. Come up here and let me work through you to draw an unbelieving world to myself. Nothing can harm you as you dwell with me from here. You will see things from my perspective. My kingdom is the kingdom of light. You will be enlightened as you dwell with me.

Stay close. I am love. I am life. I am light.

I Am that I Am that I am

Scripture:

"For God will never give you the spirit of fear, but the Holy Spirit who gives you mighty power, love, and self-control." (2 Timothy 1:7 – TPT)

"My divinely loved friends, since you are resident aliens and foreigners in this world, I appeal to you to divorce yourselves from the evil desires that wage war within you." (1 Peter 2:11 – TPT)

"... for we are now co-seated as one with Christ!" (Ephesians 2:6 - TPT)

"PURPOSED FOR MY APPOINTED TIME"

My Question:

Who are the 24 Elders in the book of Revelation?

His Answer:

They are hierarchal and have been with me from the beginning of time. They've been the apple of my eye, and I've brooded over them as a mother hen broods over her chicks. They've been purposed for my appointed time, and nothing will stand against my purposes.

I have appointed you for such a time as this. You have a part to play in my plans, so play it well.

Your Heavenly Father and the Mighty Conqueror, I Am.

Scripture:

"…for whoever touches you touches the apple of his eye…" (Zechariah 2:8 – NIV)

"O city of Jerusalem, you are the city that murders your prophets! You are the city that pelts to death with stones the very messengers who were sent to deliver you! So many times I have longed to gather your wayward children together around me, as a hen gathers her chicks under her wings – but you were too stubborn to let me." (Luke 13:34 – TPT)

"Then I looked and heard the voice of many angels, numbering thousands upon thousands, and ten thousand times ten thousand. They encircled the throne and the living creatures and the elders." (Revelation 5:11 – NIV)

(A commentary by Charles Capps Ministries said John saw the 24 elders who represent the Old and New Testament saints around the throne of God singing the song of the redeemed.)

"LOVE LIKE I LOVE YOU"

My Question:

Father, how can you possibly love us as you do?

His Answer:

My love came down to love you; to a world in need of salvation. I gave all I had so that I could have all of you. You were on my mind from the beginning of time. I only created time for a time. Soon there will be no need for time. But until that time, I want you and all my children to pour the love I've poured into you back out – onto a needy people with no home in my kingdom. I have plenty of room in my kingdom – room for many who are homeless, needy, lonely and in distress - without peace. Bring them into my kingdom. Show them the way by pouring out the love I've given you.

I want you to love like I love you.

Your Loving Father, I Am

Scripture:

"Fasten your hearts to the love of God and receive the mercy of our Lord Jesus Christ, who gives us eternal life. Keep being compassionate to those who still have doubts, and snatch others out of the fire to save them. Be merciful over and over to them, but always couple your mercy with the fear of God. Be extremely careful to keep yourselves free from the pollutions of the flesh. Now, to the one with enough power to prevent you from stumbling into sin and bring you faultless before his glorious presence to stand before him with ecstatic delight, to the only God our Savior, through our Lord Jesus Christ, be endless glory and majesty, great power and authority - from before he created time, now and throughout all the ages of eternity. Amen!" (Jude 1:21-25 – TPT)

"I love each of you with the same love that the Father loves me." (John 15:9 - TPT)

"HEAR MY VOICE"

My Question:

What is your desire, Lord?

His Answer:

Oh how I delight in you my dear children – you who long to hear my voice. My desire is that you would long to hear my voice. I have a plan and purpose for each of you. You are my design. I made you and fashioned you for my purposes. Tune in to me. Give me your ear so that you will hear my voice. I know the plans I have for you.

I want you to discover the destiny I've placed in you so that you will move when I tell you to, and be still when I say to be still. I want you to know when to speak and the words I want you to say. Effectual words launched at the right time will bear much fruit.

Dig out your ears and purpose in your hearts to hear my voice. I will lead you and guide you in the way you should go. I want each of you to live out the very destiny I've placed in you. You have purpose, just as my Son who came to earth had purpose.

Set your sight on me and I will lead and guide you. Keep your eyes on me. My glory and grace will find its resting place in you. My light will shine from you and light up the darkest places and bring hope – hope to thirsty souls and a weary world.

Keep your eyes on me and hear me when I call to you. I love you with a ferocious love and long for you to hear my voice. I love you. Your loving Father, I Am

Scripture:

"For I know the plans I have for you, declares the Lord, plans to prosper you and not to harm you, plans to give you hope and a future. Then you will call on me and come and pray to me, and I will listen to you. You will seek me and find me when you seek me with all your heart. I will be found by you, declares the Lord…" (Jeremiah 29:11-14 – TPT)

"COMMUNE WITH ME"

My Question:

Father, you said "give me your ear" in 2019. So, I am listening, and will be intentional in hearing you. What would you have to say to me today?

His Answer:

Uninterrupted worship – this is what I desire of you – flowing from your lips and heart. Remember me. I am with you always and will never leave you. Remember I am with you wherever you go. I am training you to listen for me. When you hear my voice, you will know it is me, for my sheep know my voice.

Commune with me. Communing with me is one of the highest forms of worship – for it delights my heart and satisfies my desires. Come with me to the mountaintops of praise. My kingdom holds the atmosphere of praise. Worship me on my high and holy hill. There, my refreshment and supply will be found.

Your inheritance is here with me, so remember me and come to me often. Let praise and worship pour from your lips. It is like the taste of honey, the scent of all of nature, the touch of love.

Behold, I am coming soon – but until I return for you, let my Spirit and my Word be your continual guide. Let your words and your life be a continual sacrifice of praise to me.

Your Heavenly Father, I Am

Scripture:

Deuteronomy 31:6; Joshua 1:5; Revelation 3:11; Revelation 22:12; Revelation 22:7; Revelation 22:20

"…As I was with Moses, so I will be with you; I will never leave you nor forsake you." (Joshua 1:5 – NIV)

"My own sheep will hear my voice and I know each one, and they will follow me. I give to them the gift of eternal life and they will never be lost and no one has the power to snatch them out of my hands." (John 10:27,28 – TPT)

"CO-SEATED WE WILL ALWAYS BE"

My Question:

A dear friend and sister in the Lord is nearing her destiny to come to you and your kingdom – her heavenly dwelling place. I asked: Jesus, are you coming for our friend today, or are you going to let her stay a little longer?

His Answer:

She has and always will be with me. Whether on earth or in Heaven, there is no separation in me. She always has been and will continue to be my daughter, my delight. She has been and will continue to be seated with me in the heavenly realms – in Me. Co-seated we will always be – throughout all eternity.

I have many plans and eternal purposes for all who put their trust in me. This world is passing away, yet I am making all things new.

I Am

Scripture:

"He raised us up with Christ the exalted One, and we ascended with him into the glorious perfection and authority of the heavenly realm, for we are now co-seated as one with Christ!" (Ephesians 2:6 – TPT)

"This world and its desires are in the process of passing away, but those who love to do the will of God live forever." (1 John 2:17 – TPT)

"He will wipe away every tear from their eyes and eliminate death entirely. No one will mourn or weep any longer. The pain of wounds will no longer exist, for the old order has ceased." (Revelation 21:4 – NIV)

"Behold, I'm standing at the door, knocking. If your heart is open to hear my voice and you open the door within, I will come in to you and feast with you, and you will feast with me. And to the one who conquers I will give the privilege of sitting with me on my throne, just as I conquered and sat down with my Father on his throne." (Revelation 4:20,21 – TPT)

"When one of God's holy lovers dies, it is costly to the Lord, touching His heart. (Psalm 116:15 - TPT)

"APPLY MY BLOOD AND LIVE"

My Question:

Lord, tell me more about your blood.

His Answer:

Life is in the blood. Your life co-mingled with mine. As you take of the cup, you are mixing my blood with yours, reminding you of the very covenant I made with you. My covenant is my promise to you and all who are mine - an everlasting promise. I take no prisoners captive. All who freely come to me are mine.

As my Father sees you, he sees you complete in me. That is why you are able to boldly come to him. In you, he sees me. I am your covering, the only covering you will ever need. I am like your receiving blanket. The Father receives you because you are "wrapped in me". (Ahhh, the smell of my Son!)

My blood is provision for everything you will ever need. Apply my blood often. Apply it to all you put your hand to. Apply it to yourselves, your spouses, your children and children's children. Apply it to your homes and modes of transportation. Apply it daily – early in the morning. Satan cannot touch anything with my blood on it. My blood is life – shed for you so that you would have the abundant life I spoke of in John 10:10. Satan, your adversary, cannot steal, kill or destroy when my covenant blood is applied. Use the authority I have given you and apply my blood and live.

Scripture:

"Then taking the cup of wine and giving praises to the Father, he entered into covenant with them saying, "This is my blood. Each of you must drink it in fulfillment of the covenant. For this is the blood that seals the new covenant. It will be poured out for many for the complete forgiveness of sins." (Matthew 26:27,28 – TPT)

"…We come to him for mercy, for God has made a provision for us to be forgiven by faith in the sacred blood of Jesus…" (Romans 3:25 – TPT)

"And there is still much more to say of his unfailing love for us! For through the blood of Jesus we have heard the powerful declaration, "You are now righteous in my sight." And because of the sacrifice of Jesus, you will never experience the wrath of God." (Romans 5:9 – TPT)

"Since we are now joined to Christ, we have been given the treasures of redemption by his blood – the total cancellation of our sins – all because of the cascading riches of his grace." (Ephesians 1:7 – TPT)

"Yet look at you now! Everything is new! Although you were once distant and far away from God, now you have been brought delightfully close to him through the sacred blood of Jesus – you have actually been united to Christ!" (Ephesians 2:13 – TP)

"THERE IS PEACE IN MY PRESENCE"

Father, I am feeling weary. I need to hear your voice.

His Response:

Peace –

Be still. I will strengthen you and give you what you need. In times of distress, lean on me. I am your strength and comforter. Come to me and I will give you rest.

Do not rely on your own strength. Come and let me dandle you on my knee. I know everything about you. I see you. You are never out of my sight. Let me never be out of yours. I am reliable and ready to help in your time of need.

As you become aware of my presence, my glory and shalom peace will find you. I long for you to live here in my presence, now and for all eternity. My presence will never leave you nor forsake you. You are the one who leaves and forsakes me at times, but I will always be here with and for you. In my presence there is strength. In my presence there is peace. Come out from the storms of life and come into my presence where nothing can harm you.

Remember me always. Remember me often. Remember me, for "I Am" your peace!

I Am

Scripture:

"Above the furious flood, the Enthroned One reigns, the King-God rules with eternity at his side. This is the one who gives his strength and might to his people. This is the Lord giving us his kiss of peace." (Psalm 29:10,11 – TPT)

"He gives strength to the weary and increases the power of the weak... those who hope in the Lord will renew their strength. They will soar on wings like eagles; they will run and not grow weary, they will walk and not be faint." (Isaiah 41:29-31 - NIV)

"I SEE YOU"

My Question:

This morning I was reading Psalm 78. " …So quickly they wandered away from his promises, following God with their words and not their hearts." You Look upon the heart, don't you Lord?

His Answer:

I desire the hearts of all mankind. I desire to dwell in each one. Out of the heart flows the issues of life. I see you. I see each heart laid bare before me. I see the hearts that truly want me to come in and live, where I can reach into the world through them to make a difference in the lives of others. I see the hearts bowed low before me – intimately loving and desiring more of me.

Let not your hearts be troubled, for I have overcome the world. Do not let fear trouble your hearts. Nor doubt. I have given you a spirit of power, love and a sound mind. Do not allow the issues of this troubled world enter your hearts. Come up here and look to me for your help, your hope and your supply. This is your true home and dwelling place.

Pray for your brothers and sisters who need a strengthening of heart and who need an awakening of heart – awakened toward me. And, pray for those whose hearts are cold and closed toward me. Pray their stony hearts become softened and that they would have ears to hear and eyes to see.

The door is open. Time is short. I desire all people to come to me, for my love is for all. Work with me and pray – for I am coming soon.

I Am

Scripture:

"A good man brings good things out of the good stored up in him, and an evil man brings evil things out of the evil stored up in him." (Matthew 12:35 – NIV)

"Don't worry or surrender to your fear. For you've believed in God, now trust and believe in me also." (John 14:1 – TPT)

"I leave the gift of peace with you – my peace. Not the kind of fragile peace given by the world, but my perfect peace. Don't yield to fear or be troubled in your hearts – instead be courageous!" (John 14:27 – TPT)

"WITH GOD, ALL THINGS ARE POSSIBLE"

My Question:

What will this New Year bring, Lord?

His Answer:

This New Year – 2022 – is pregnant with all kinds of possibilities! Remember, with God, all things are possible.

What you thought was impossible or improbable will become possible and probable with me. I turn water into wine, sickness into healing, blindness into sight. I turn the tables upside down and resurrect those things that you thought were dead.

I am your protector, your healer, your defense. Unholy schemes and plots and plans cannot stop my plans that I have purposed. There is none like me!

I am about to step into the scene in ways you have not known or could even imagine. My ways are higher than yours. I am about to give birth to my plans! I am past due. I have held back, purposing for all to come to repentance. I've given my gift of more time, but it's about to run out. The tables are about to turn. Watch and see, for there is none like me!

I Am

Scripture:

"As the heavens are higher than the earth, so are my ways higher than your ways and my thoughts than your thoughts." (Isaiah 55:9 – NIV)

"Jesus looked at them and said, "With man this is impossible, but with God all things are possible." (Matthew 19:26 – NIV)

"So Jesus found some rope and made it into a whip. Then he drove out every one of them and their animals from the courtyard of the temple, and he kicked over their tables filled with money, scattering it everywhere! And he shouted at the merchants, "Get these things out of here! Don't you dare make my Father's house into a center for merchandise!" (John 2:15,16 – TPT)

"A RESERVED PLACE FOR YOU"

My Question:

(Psalm 25:14 – TPT) "There is a private place reserved for the lovers of God, where they sit near him and receive the revelation-secrets of his promises." Lord, will you speak to me about this scripture?

His Answer:

Like a dinner reservation, there is a reserved place for you to come and meet with me. Reserved for my lovers, those who long to come and spend time with me. I created you for this very reason – that you would come to me and love on me as I love on you. To share my ways with you. To share my very word with you.

My word is pregnant with good things. Oh come, taste and see my goodness. You are a sweet smelling aroma to me. I share my glory with all who are mine.

My Spirit longs to dance with you. Take my hand and let me lead you. Let me hold you close. Let me gaze into your eyes and touch your heart with my love – my undying love. Yes, I died for you with an undying love. Come close and let me reveal more of my love for you. Keep coming, for there's no end to my love. It is eternal.

I Am more than enough.

I AM

Scripture:

"Drink deeply of the pleasures of this God. Experience for yourself the joyous mercies he gives to all who turn to hide themselves in him. Worship in awe and wonder, all you who've been made holy! For all who fear him will feast with plenty." (Psalm 34:8,9 – TPT)

"…We will dance in the high place of the sky, yes, on the mountains of fragrant spice. Forever we shall be united as one!" (Song of Songs 8:14 – TPT)

… "How deeply intimate and far-reaching is His love! How enduring and inclusive it is! Endless love beyond measurement that transcends our understanding - this extravagant love pours into you until you are filled to overflowing with the fullness of God." (Ephesians 3:18,19 - TPT)

"I LOVE YOU"

The Lord said to me in my spirit as I was ending this work: (and this was for all of you!!!)

"I LOVE YOU WITH A LOVE THAT WILL NEVER DIE."

Scripture:

"Who could ever separate us from the endless love of God's Anointed One? Absolutely no one! For nothing in the universe has the power to diminish his love toward us. Troubles, pressures and problems are unable to come between us and heaven's love. What about persecutions, deprivations, dangers, and death threats? No for they are all impotent to hinder omnipotent love, even though it is written: All day long we face death threats for your sake, God. We are considered to be nothing more than sheep to be slaughtered! Yet even in the midst of all these things, we triumph over them all, for God has made us to be more than conquerors, and his demonstrated love is our glorious victory over everything!" (Romans 8:35-39 – TPT)

"…Because His heart was focused on the joy of knowing that you would be His, He endured the agony of the cross and conquered its humiliation, and now sits exalted at the right hand of the throne of God." (Hebrews 12:2 – TPT)

"I pray that the Father of glory, the God of our Lord Jesus Christ, would impart to you the riches of the Spirit of wisdom and the Spirit of revelation to know him (Jesus) through your deepening intimacy with him." (Ephesians 1:17 – TPT)

"…How deeply intimate and far-reaching is his love! How enduring and inclusive it is! Endless love beyond measurement that transcends our understanding – this extravagant love pours into you until you are filled to the overflowing of the fullness of God." (Ephesians 3:18,19 – TPT)

These blank pages are provided for your notes and for you to journal with the Lord, if you desire to do so.

_____

_____

_____

_____

_____

_____

_____

_____

_____

_____

_____

_____

_____

_____

_____

_____

_____

_____

_____

www.ingramcontent.com/pod-product-compliance
Lightning Source LLC
Chambersburg PA
CBHW051542120626
46551CB00013B/1335